THE

M-TRAWL FISHERY OF GREAT BRITA

AND

NOTES ON BEAM-TRAWLING IN OTHER EUROPEAN COUNTRIES.

BY

J. W. COLLINS.

WASHINGTON
GOVERNMENT PRINTING OFFICE
1889

60. THE BEAM-TRAWL FISHERY OF GREAT BRITAIN, WITH NOTES ON BEAM-TRAWLING IN OTHER EUROPEAN COUNTRIES, ETC.

BY J. W. COLLINS

A INTRODUCTORY NOTE

This report has been prepared for the purpose of placing before those directly interested in the fisheries of the United States such information as seems necessary to convey a moderately comprehensive idea of the British beam-trawl fishery. The history, development, and importance of this special branch of the fisheries in European waters have been dwelt upon at some length. Attention has been called to the possible influence of the beam trawl on the abundance of fish, and the question of the introduction of this form of apparatus into the fisheries of the United States has been discussed

But in view of the possible employment of the beam trawl for the capture of fish in American waters special attention has been given to the various details of its construction. It has also been deemed desirable, for the same reason, to describe at length the various forms of apparatus which are used in conjunction with the trawl, as well as the methods of fishing, the system of marketing the catch, and other matters relating to the prosecution of the work in Europe, since a knowl edge of these details will be required by American fishermen should they ever undertake to prosecute the beam-trawl fishery.

Less has been said concerning those subjects which seem to suggest little that may be of practical value, and for this reason much has been omitted which might perhaps appropriately be included in a report of this kind. For instance, the notes on the trawl fisheries of France, Belgium, Holland, Germany, and Spain might have been expanded to a greater extent, but it is believed that these contain all the data which may be of any importance to fishing companies in the United States.

It is proper that acknowledgments should be made to the following gentlemen, who have lent their aid in various ways, but more particularly in furnishing such information as is required for a work of this character. Foremost among those who have assisted by their kindly efforts are Mr. Harrison Mudd and Mr. O. T. Olsen, of Grimsby, Mr. Edward Fox, of London, and Mr. T. J. Robinson Curr, of North Shields, while others have furnished much interesting and valuable data concerning the British beam-trawl fisheries.

Mons. A. Duchochois, of Boulogne, has supplied data relative to the French beam-trawl fisheries. Mons. Jules Le Lorrain, of Belgium, has furnished many important facts concerning the fisheries prosecuted from that country. I am also indebted to Mr. A. E. Maas, of Scheveningen, for information relative to the Dutch trawl fishery.

The material upon which this report is based was chiefly gathered at Grimsby and Hull, and during a trip to the North Sea in 1880, also from a study of apparatus and methods at the International Fisheries Exposition at London in 1883. So far as I am informed, however, there has been little if any change since the last mentioned date, beyond perhaps the introduction of additional steam vessels in the beam-trawl fishery from the continental ports.

I.—THE BEAM-TRAWL FISHERY OF GREAT BRITAIN

B.—HISTORY AND PRESENT IMPORTANCE

Nothing definite can now be learned as to where or when the method of fishing with a beam-trawl in Great Britain originated. Undoubtedly trawl nets of some kind have been in use for many centuries on the English coast, but there remain no records which would suggest that they were supplied with a beam to distend their mouths, and as the most primitive and oldest forms of trawl nets now in use are unprovided with beams, it is probable that those first employed in England were of this type.

The earliest notice which we can find of the trawl fishery in England is contained in the following petition, which was presented to Parliament in 1376–77.[1]

[1] It will be noticed that there is nothing in this petition to indicate the use of beams as a part of the apparatus. The term used in this connection refers to the beam-trawl or some other form is in use.

(Pet. 51 Edw. III, A. D. 1376-77.—Petition No. 50.) "That whereas in several places within your said realm, in creeks and havens of the sea, where was accustomed before these times to be a good and plenteous fishery to the great profit of the realm, which is in part destroyed and rendered valueless for a long time to come by some fishermen who have for times during seven years past by a subtlety contrived a new instrument, which is amongst themselves called a 'wondyrchoum,' made after the fashion of a drag for oysters, which is usually long, to which instrument is attached a net (*rete*) of so small a mesh no manner of fish however small entering within it can pass out, and is compelled to *remain therein and be taken*. And besides this, the hard and long iron of the said 'wondyrchoum,' that it destroys the spawn and brood of the fish beneath the said water, and also destroys the spat of oysters, muscles, and other fish by which large fish are accustomed to live and be supported. By means of which instruments called 'wondyrchoums' in many places aforesaid the fishermen aforesaid take so great abundance of small fish aforesaid that they know not what to do with them, to the great damage of the commons of the Kingdom and the destruction of the fisheries in like places. For which they pray remedy.

"*Responsio.*—Let commission be made by qualified persons, to inquire and certify on the truth of this allegation, and thereon let right be done in the court of chancery."

The fishing towns of Brixham and Barking, in their local traditions, both lay claim to the distinction of having been the first to introduce and establish the method of fishing with beam trawls, but as these claims are based solely on tradition it still remains a mooted question as to which is the most entitled to the honor. One writer has attempted to prove the probability of this method of fishing having been introduced by the Dutch on the occasion of the landing at Brixham of the Prince of Orange in 1688.

He says, however, that "for the next hundred years there was no craft employed at Brixham at fishing but open boats and half-deck yawls, the latter being the latest improvement. We have [he continues] heard our grandsires relate how they used to put the whole apparatus, or gear, as it is now called, on their back and carry it on board of the boat. * * * Shortly after this time the fishermen began to enlarge their crafts, to cover in the deck fore and aft, and rig them as cutters—namely, boom, gaff, and bowsprit, and with topmast having a long pole on which was set a royal with the sheets leading down on deck, the same as the Dutch Schevling bomhs of the present day, and most probably the rig was taken from them."[1]

The trawl net in various forms has unquestionably been used in the continental fisheries of Europe for many years, but the application of the beam is apparently of more recent date.

---

[1] The Fisherman's Magazine, March, 1881.

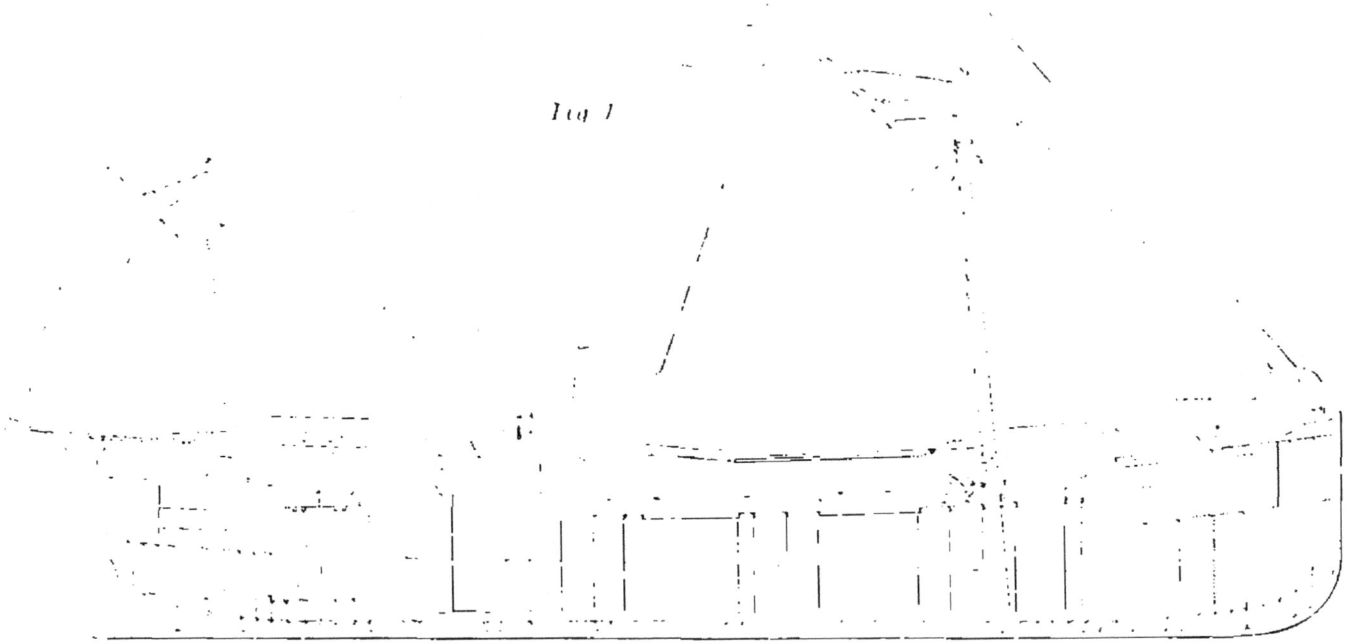

Fig 1

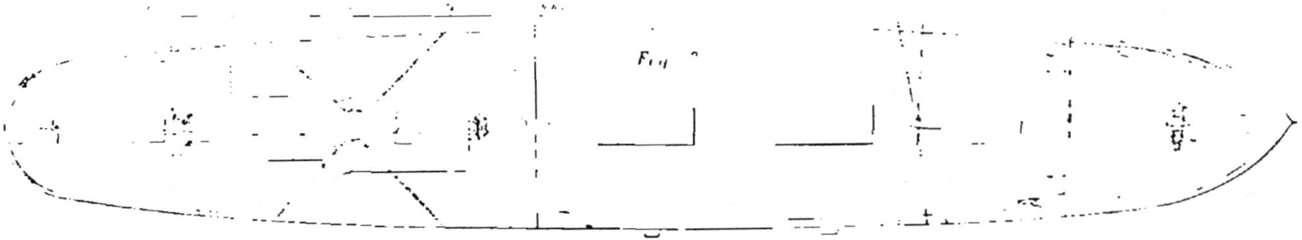

Fig 2

with remarkable rapidity until now it is considered one of the most important fisheries of the British Isles, while in England it takes precedence of all others.

The most important method of fishing, writes Holdsworth, "by which a regular supply of the best and most varied kinds of sea fish is obtained for the market is that commonly known as 'trawling'—a name evidently derived from trailing or dragging, the trawl being a bag net which is towed, trailed, or trawled along the bottom, and it is so constructed as to capture those fish especially which naturally keep upon or near the ground.

The most noted ports in England from which trawling is prosecuted are on the east coast and most of them north of the Thames. They are in the order of their importance as trawling stations Yarmouth, Grimsby, Hull, Lowestoft, London, and Scarborough; while Brixham, Rams-gate Plymouth, and Dover, in the south of England, are noted for their trawling fleets. Caernarvon and Tenby in Wales have small fleets of trawlers.

Aberdeen, Granton, and Leith, in Scotland, have each a number of trawling steamers, though Mr. T. J. Robertson Carr, writing from Edinburgh under date of August 25, 1883, says:

The General Steam Fishing Company, Limited, is the only beam trawling company of any importance in Scotland, and their headquarters are at Granton, in the Firth of Forth, close to Leith.

When Holdsworth wrote in 1874 there was no beam trawling station of any importance on the coast of Scotland. The statement is made in the First Annual Report of the Fishery Board for Scotland, 1882, that—

Beam trawling has been carried on for several years in the Moray Firth by sailing smacks and boats, principally belonging to Lossiemouth, and it has also been prosecuted for a considerable period by sailing smacks and boats in the Firth of Clyde. Beam trawling by steamers, which has been more recently adopted, has greatly increased within the last two or three years.

According to the Scotsman of December 8, 1883:

At the present moment the fleet of screw trawlers belonging to Granton numbers fifteen, and the capital thus employed in the industry here there may be roughly estimated at between £40,000 and £50,000."

Dublin, Galway, Waterford, and Dingle are the principal stations in Ireland from which large vessels are employed in trawling.

Besides all the fleets of large sailing smacks and steamers which en-

Mr. Dugald Stewart, managing director of the fishing interest of R. Allen & Co., of Grimsby, states that in 1872 Aberdeen had no screw boats and five pedal steam trawlers. One of the first and most successful trawlers who ever ... sole wheelers sailed from the ... Peter Walker, trawl-owner and skipper of Belfast, was before the first to ... seagoing surface smacks and trawling operations on the east coast of Scotland. Here are now seven sailing trawlers and one steam trawler belonging to this ... working generally from Leith Head down to Berwick. For much the ...

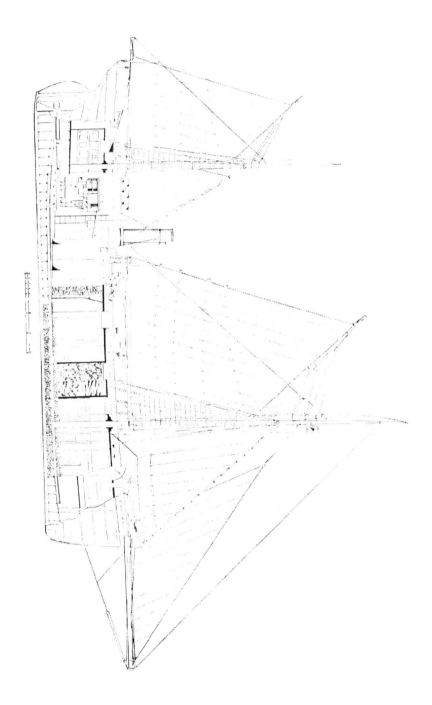

STEAM TRAWLER ZODIAC.
Sectional elevation and sail plan.

gage in this industry; more or less trawling is carried on in the shore and various parts of the coast of the British Isles by small boats, but until recently the Scotch have employed this method comparatively little, and even now other means of catching fish are generally preferred by the boat fishermen of that country.

The remarkable development of the beam-trawl fishery of the east coast of England during the past forty years, the consequent increase in the trawling fleets, and the growth and prosperity of the principal fishing ports are perhaps without a parallel in the history of the British fisheries.

Take Grimsby, for example, which about 1858, according to Mr. Harrison Mudd, a prominent citizen of that port, had a population of approximately from 10,000 to 15,000, and had just begun its career as a fishing town by sending out a few beam-trawlers, now it has increased to upwards of 30,000 inhabitants, and from its docks sail a fleet of nearly 800 fishing vessels, more than half of which are beam-trawlers. Mr. Edward Fox and other gentlemen say that they can recollect when Hull and Lowestoft (some thirty-five or forty years ago) did not have more than 25 or 30 sail of trawlers to each port. In 1884 Hull had a fleet of 757 and Lowestoft 467 vessels of all classes, the majority of which were trawlers.

"The rapid development of late years," writes Mr. Ansell, "may be traced to the introduction of ice and the spread of our railway system, by which the catcher has been enabled to get the fruits of his toil distributed to the many thousands dwelling in the inland towns—those who seldom or never saw or tasted salt-water fish."

It may also be added that the introduction of the method of icing fish has given the trawlers an opportunity, which they have not been slow to improve, to visit distant and untried grounds where fish could be taken in much greater abundance than nearer home.

According to Mr. Ansell the advance of the trawling trade was so rapid on the east coast that Hull, which in 1845 had only 21 vessels aggregating 570 tons, and valued at £6,425, had, in 1882-'83 increased its fleet to 447 smacks, besides 9 steam-cutters and 9 ice-ships, with a tonnage of 29,233 tons, and a valuation of £755,000.

Still more remarkable has been the growth of the beam-trawl fishery from Grimsby. It was first introduced, according to Holdsworth, in 1858, at which time 5 smacks went there from Hull. The rapid strides which this fishery has made at that port may be judged from the fact that the amount of fish landed there had increased from 1,441 tons in 1858 to over 73,000 tons in 1881, while we are credibly informed that about 100,000 tons were landed in 1882-'83. Though all of these fish were not caught in beam-trawls a large percentage were so taken, and it is perhaps not too much to assume that the increase in the fisheries

Papers of the Conferences held in connection with the Great International Fisheries Exhibition, London, 1883. On Trawling, by Alfred W. Ansell.

of Grimsby is due more to the advance made in beam trawling than to anything else. Besides the fish landed at Grimsby, large quantities caught by trawlers fishing from that port go by water in steam carriers to London.

As to the present status and importance of the British beam trawl fishery, Mr. Ansell makes the following interesting statements:

The number of British deep-sea trawlers may be taken at 3,000 (not including steam cutters). Yarmouth leading with 700, Hull and Grimsby next, making together about half the number, the rest being scattered round our coasts. Such smacks as sail from Yarmouth, Hull, and Grimsby fetches is the deepest trawler. Taking the average catch of each of these at 100 tons brings the total weight to 300,000 tons, irrespective of the inshore trawlers catches as in the case of Hull and Grimsby, and also Messrs. Hewitts, and others less of course, and more prime. We may take an estimate of £8 to £12 per ton as the price it fetches. This will give us a total money value of fish caught by the deep-sea trawlers of £2,400,000 at £10, or £3,600,000 at £12.

The Duke of Edinburgh, in a paper read at the conferences at the London International Fisheries Exhibition, entitled "Sea Fisheries and Fishing Populations," makes a more moderate and probably a more accurate estimate. He places the total production by this method in the British Isles at 214,157 tons, worth £2,581,000, equal to about £2,500,000.

He continues Ansell, we take capital employed in producing this at a total of £3,000,000 invested in floating and shore property, it is not over-estimating it. We have the ships, ice-houses, steam carriers, curing-houses, salting-houses, and many other things too numerous to mention. The number of hands to man these vessels, at five or six hands per ship (though some carry more) makes from 15,000 to 18,000, the latter is more like the number. If to this we add 2,000 who are out of berth, or changing ships, we have then 20,000 hardy and experienced hands employed in deep-sea trawling, and who have no other calling or occupation. Some of these have families, and others living, presumably in each ship to be married with each a wife and four children; we have 30,000 more who are altogether dependent on the trawl for support. But as the trade cannot be carried on without assistance of shore labor, it gives employment to many more such as packers, carters, laborers, watchmen, coopers, net-makers, riggers, etc., and a vast number of other trades too numerous to mention."

C. FISHING GROUNDS

The North Sea or German Ocean from the Straits of Dover to Kinnaird's Head on the Scottish coast, and the Skager Rack, on the continental side, is the most favorable field for the prosecution of the beam trawl fishery. Within the area mentioned the water is generally shallow, varying from 5 to 15 fathoms, upwards of 50 fathoms, and may be

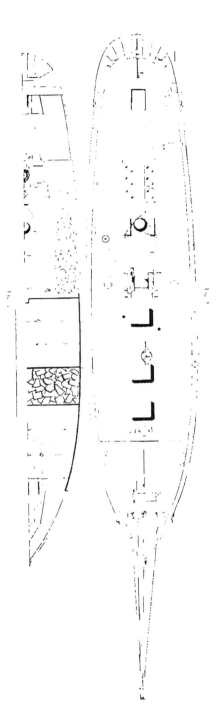

PLANS OF STEAM TRAWLER ZODIAC

Fig. 1. Profile and profile plan with deck and section 1 showing internal arrangement

PLATE III

considered one vast fishing bank, though there are various parts of greater or less extent in this part of the North Sea that are specially noted trawling grounds, and to which specific names have been given.

A bottom of mud or sand, in a moderate depth of water, is the most favorable ground for the use of the beam trawl, providing, of course, fish can be taken thereon; but it often happens that fish are much more abundant on rocky grounds, known by the name of "roughs" among the North Sea fishermen. Therefore, though there is always a great risk of losing the trawl when working on rough bottom, the hope of obtaining a large catch is often sufficient inducement for the fishermen to make the venture.

The most noted of the North Sea fishing grounds is the Dogger Bank, divided into several sections which are distinguished by local names—the Off Ground, the Great Silver Pits, Botney Ground, Brown Bank, the Coast, Leman Ground, and the Great Fisher Bank. Besides these, mention may be made of the Horn Reef, Jutland Reef, Flamborough Head Ground, Scarborough Ground, Hartlepool Ground, Sunderland Ground, Flinch Ground, the Cemetery Flat or Well Bank, Sole Pit or Northeast Hole, Smiths Knowl Ground, Knowl or Dowsing Ground, the South Ground, North Foreland Ground, Kentish Knock Ground, Margate Ground, the New Bank or Sandettie, the Falls Ground, Ridge and Varn Banks, and Rye Bay.

"The fishing grounds most frequented by vessels from the Humber [Hull and Grimsby]," writes Mr. Ansell, "are the shoal of the Dogger, the southwest and northwest spot of the Dogger, Clay Deeps, the northeast part of the Dogger called the Cemetery [from the rough stony nature of the bottom compared to grave stones], the Fisher Bank, and beyond the Fisher Bank, Jutland Reefs, the Long Forties, the Horn Reefs, the Sylt, the Amrum Bank, Heligoland, off the entrance of the Weser and Elbe, Nordeney, Borkum, Terschelling, Texel, etc., besides other grounds south of the Humber, such as the Wells Bank, etc. * * *

"Plaice are to be found only in the spring and fall on the shoal of the Dogger, and in summer on the Horn Reef and Borkum. In winter, below the Dogger and off the Flamborough Head.

"Haddocks are found in abundance on the southwest spot of the Dogger about October; in September and October they work along the pit edge of the Dogger, and when taken they are found to have plenty of herring and spawn in them.

"Soles are caught on hard sandy ground in warm weather, taking to deep water such as the pits, where the bottom is muddy and soft, in winter, for warmth."

The Dogger Bank which is a very extensive ground is situated nearly in the middle of the North Sea, its southwest prong is about 70 miles in an east northeast direction from Spurn Point at the mouth of the Humber. From there it extends northeastwardly a distance of 150 miles ending in a point. It is somewhat irregular in form, being about 60 miles wide in the broadest place. Different parts of the Dogger are known by specific names among the fishermen. The "West Shoal" which is a shallow ground on the southwest part of the bank, is about 20 miles long ESE and WNW with a depth of from 7 to 10 fathoms and a fine sandy bottom. Then there is the "Outer Well Bank," or the "Southwest Spot" with from 15 to 18 fathoms, with a bottom of fine sand and occasional spots of coarse sand and small rocks. In this locality haddock and plaice are frequently found in abundance during the fall. Between the Southwest spot and the West Shoal the shallow part of the bank curves inwardly like a cove, with irregular soundings, varying from 20 to 10 fathoms. On what is known as the south part of the bank east of the West Shoal the bottom is chiefly fine sand, with a depth of from 11 to 20 fathoms. This is a good fishing ground, and is much visited. The "East End" in latitude 55°25′ north, longitude 4°40′ east, is noted for fine brown sandy bottom, free from what the fishermen call scruff or rubbish, the depth varying from 22 to 24 fathoms. This is now considered one of the best fishing grounds on the Dogger. To the southwest, in latitude 54°50′ north, longitude 3°20′ east is the "Clay Deep" or "Southeast Swish of Dogger Bank" of soft ooze, 25 miles long southwest and northeast with rough ground on either side. The "North Shoal" and "Northwest Spot" are tracks of more or less rough bottom.

The Great Silver Pits, the west end of which lies due east of Spurn Point some 60 miles distant, is a gully or depression of the sea bottom between the Dogger Bank on the NNE and Wells Bank on the opposite side. Its length east and west is about 40 miles and its width varies from 10 to 14 miles. The depth ranges from 25 to about 50 fathoms, with patches of bottom of different kinds such as black mud, fine sand, white mud, blue clay, stones, and gravel.

This celebrated fishing ground was discovered about 1843, and on it soles were found in extraordinary abundance. It still is a favorite resort in winter for such of the trawlers as fish more particularly for soles.

The Great Fisher Bank is thus described by Olsen:

This large space of ground known by the name of the Great Fisher Bank, is situated in the northeast part of the German Ocean. It is of vast extent, and has recently been discovered as a trawling ground. The ground chiefly consists of sandy soundings of mud and ooze, with depths of water varying from 40 to 45 fathoms.

In Longshore Fishing News Chronicle, published by Asher & Co., London [illegible]. When the Silver Pits were first discovered it was not an uncommon thing for a trawler to get a ton and a half of soles a night of from £12 to £24 value.
Olsen says: Large quantities of soles were caught for the first three years.

When the Silver Pits were first discovered, writes Ansell, and became the greatest of all fishing grounds the sole was so abundant in winter months in such enormous quantities that the name Silver Pits was to the fisher not the name thing only, so prospered were those shoresorts. [illegible]

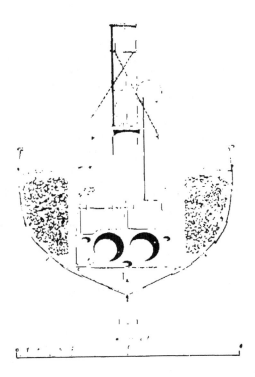

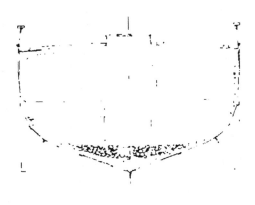

PLAN OF STEAM TRAWLER ZODIAC

The best track hitherto used ... 1877, is in latitude 57° 20' north and longitude 1° 40' east ... As the bank is of recent discovery as a trawling ground it is not considered as yet to be fully explored, but we find that the eastern part is soft, more or less, and that the north western part is most productive. Large quantities of fish, chiefly haddocks, plaice, and cod being taken hither from here to the Hull and Grimsby markets. This ground has now already been worked about 5 years.[*]

The Cromer Knoll, first fished on about 1858 lies north of the Leman and Dover Sands, between them and the Dowsing Bank. It has a depth varying from 12 to 18 fathoms, with generally a clean bottom for trawling, on which when first discovered the more highly prized species of the North Sea fishes were found in abundance.

The foregoing will give a general idea of the most important North Sea trawling grounds, which, for the purposes of this report, it seems scarcely necessary to describe in greater detail.

Areas of bottom suitable for fishing with a beam trawl of greater or less extent are found along the coast of the continent, near the east coast of Scotland, in the English Channel, along the west side of England, and off the coasts of Wales and Ireland, but they are too numerous to mention even by name in this place. Suffice it to say that the southern and western grounds have generally been worked much longer than the majority of those in the North Sea, and in general characteristics such as depth, kind of bottom, etc., they are like the latter, though as a rule of less extent.

The kind of fish chiefly taken on the above mentioned grounds are turbot, sole, brill, plaice, lemon or cock sole, dabs, and halibut of the *Pleuronectidæ*, or flat fish family, cod, haddock, hake, ling, and whiting of the *Gadidæ*, besides which conger eels, wolf fish, skates, gurnards, and a variety of other less important species are caught.

At first, previous to the introduction of ice for preserving fish, the grounds nearest the British coast were the only ones which could be fished on, and trawling was then carried on chiefly in the English Channel from Dover to Land's End, and along the coasts of Wales and Ireland. With improved methods for preserving the fish in a fresh condition, the smacks were enabled to venture further in pursuit of new and richer fields for carrying on their operations. In this way they continued to discover new fishing grounds either by accident or design, until at the present time it is pretty safe to say that there is little

Fishermen's Nomenclature List, Fisheries Exhibit. Lit. U. S. Fish. Com. for 1884, p. 16.

According to Mr. J. Fennel Carter ... the assessment of Mount's Bay, the Plymouth and Brixham trawlers fished ... that is known as the ... Brixham Ground and from there round to Mount's Bay ... Mount's Bay ... says are and the species of flat fish with ... is not taken where soles fish are chiefly caught off Brixham and Plymouth though with ... or less ... other flat fish are taken. Hake are often found in abundance.

of the bottom of the North Sea suitable for trawling, over which a beam trawl has not passed. Mr. Ansell thus describes what may be termed, perhaps, the accidental discovery of a new fishing ground some forty years ago though it may more properly be said that this find was a happy combination of chance and enterprise which so frequently influences the welfare of mankind.

Chance brought about one of the most astonishing results in the history of the fishing trade about the year 1844, and founded the trade at Hull in consequence. One of the Ramsgate boats in extending her searches for fish was by adverse winds blown further north than it was the intention of the crew, but determined to make a try, they shot their trawl in what is now so well known as the Silver Pits, and their plucky venture and labor were rewarded by a marvelous draught of fishes, which were nearly all soles. Very soon this became noised abroad and other boats followed, who were equally rewarded with good results.

According to Holdsworth, the Great Silver Pit was first worked over about 1843, during a severe winter.

The Well Bank and Botany Gut, he writes, had been explored and discovered to be very productive grounds, and between them and the Dogger, and bearing nearly due east from Flamborough Head, the Admiralty chart showed a bed of deeper soundings, ranging in some parts of it from 30 to 40 fathoms, the whole extending for about 60 miles east and west and from 6 to 10 miles wide. This patch was marked the "Outer Silver Pit," and on trying it with a trawl in the deeper parts at the western end and near the middle, soles were found during that very cold season in almost incredible numbers; the nets were hauled up bursting with fish trying to escape through the meshes, and such catches were made as the most experienced fishermen had never dreamed of. * * * In subsequent years the Silver Pit has again been found very productive whenever the winter has been very severe, or as the trawlers call it, in the seasons.

The same author tells us, however, that soles are generally distributed wherever there is clean sandy ground, but they are not found so much in very deep water except during cold weather. The London market is principally supplied with this fish from the banks of the Norfolk coast and from the Channel. * * * It is rarely that any number of soles is landed at Hull, and the Grimsby shops are often supplied from London.

D. THE FISHERMEN

The crew of a beam trawler varies from four to seven persons on a sailing vessel, and from six to eight on a steamer. The cutters of the south of England, from Plymouth, Brixham, Ramsgate, Dover, and other ports, which vary in size from 25 to 50 tons, usually carry four persons in a crew, one or more being boys. Many of the Yarmouth vessels, if not the majority of them, have seven in a crew, but the trawl

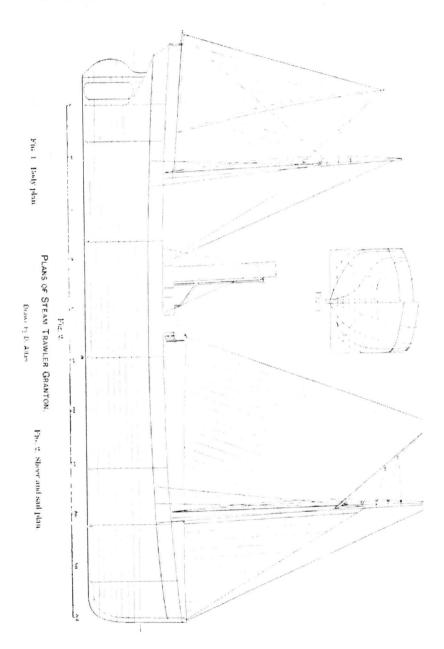

Fig. 1 Body plan

PLANS OF STEAM TRAWLER GRANTON.

Fig. 2

Drawn by D. Allan

Fig. 2 Sheer and sail plan

ers sailing from Hull and Grimsby, and which are the largest vessels of their class, carry only five persons in a crew, as a rule, though in exceptional cases the crew list may be larger.

The Grimsby steam trawlers carry eight in a crew, but the smaller class of steamers do not require so many men.

In any case, a number of boys are usually carried. The Grimsby sailing trawler generally has two boys in its crew, and sometimes the three youngest members of a crew are mere lads varying in age from twelve to seventeen years, in which case there would be only two men on board a vessel—the captain and second hand. Ordinarily the crew of a sailing trawler of the larger class is constituted as follows. The cook is the youngest, and is usually from twelve to sixteen years of age. The fourth hand, or deck hand, the next in grade, is a lad of fifteen to eighteen years of age, and generally one who has served a term at cooking. Next in rank is the third hand, who according to his ability and experience may be promoted to this position when he is from seventeen to eighteen years old, and may have to hold it for lack of further promotion for several years, the older third hands varying from seventeen to twenty-seven years of age. The "second hand" occupies the position next to the master, his duty and general position corresponding with that of a mate on a merchant vessel.

The skipper completes the crew. In almost every case promotions are made from the next lower grade, and with comparatively few exceptions the officers of a smack have served their apprenticeship in all the inferior grades. Of course there is much difference in the length of time men may have to serve before rising to command; this depending on their ability, and perhaps on other circumstances.

The duties of the various members of a trawler crew are thus demand. The cook, or, as he is sometimes called, the "fifth hand," must cook the food for all hands, and take care of the cabin and stores room where the provisions are kept. He must learn to steer by the compass, for he must take the helm while the trawl is being shot. He must also acquire a knowledge of making and mending nets and netting, take care of the fishing gear, and keep it in its proper place, and it is his duty to coil away the trawl warp when the trawl is being hove up. Also he is expected, with the assistance of the deck hand, to prepare the lights and flares for use, and to see that they are in their proper places, while the spare pump gear and fog signals must receive similar attention. As may be easily surmised, it is no easy task for a small boy of twelve or thirteen years of age to properly perform the several duties, particularly in rough weather, when the energies of a strong man would be severely taxed to do the work which is allotted to the cook. But it is sometimes wonderful to observe what may be done by a mere child who has been trained to the work, and we are told that these boy cooks generally perform their duties satisfactorily, though of course there is much less refinement in the preparation of food than on American fishing vessels.

where the cook usually receives the highest pay of any one of the crew, the captain excepted, and must be a capable and active man.

"The 'deck hand,' or 'fourth hand,' is generally a lad who has served as cook and has been promoted a grade. Therefore, he is supposed to be able to do all that the cook can do besides the special duties belonging to his new position. The deck hand must know how to steer and keep a watch in fine weather when sailing or trawling. To do this, he must be able to manage a vessel under ordinary conditions of wind and weather.

"He should be able to manage a boat in fine weather, know the marks of the lead line and take soundings, splice small ropes and whip them, make nettles, gaskets, or sennet, braid a cod end, and learn to mend small holes in the net. He ought to tend the trawl in fine weather, keep the hold and forecastle clean and in proper order, know the sails by the marks [the sails are known by pieces of twine with knots on the end][1] in the dark, and keep them in their proper places, make thole-pins for the trawl warp, rail and boat, help to prepare fish for the market, assist the cook to trim lights, and obey all lawful commands.

"The 'third hand' rates as an ordinary seaman, and usually has passed through the two lower grades. He should have sufficient experience to manage a vessel when her trawl is out as well as at other times; must be capable of keeping the ordinary long watches, which on a trawler may be six or eight hours on deck, and he must understand the 'rules of the road,' so as to avoid collision. It is required that he should learn the set of the tides, take soundings, understand how to make, mend, rig, and prepare a trawl for shooting; also it is a part of his duty to go in the boat when fish are to be 'boarded' or taken to the carrier, while he is expected to have a care for the rigging, put on chafing gear, etc., besides assisting in the care of the fish.

"The mate, or 'second hand,' should be an able seaman, and be more thoroughly conversant with the general work than the third hand. It is important that he should have a very comprehensive knowledge of all that pertains to making a trawl, preparing the bridles, shooting the gear, managing the smack under all conditions of wind and weather, either sailing or fishing, while he ought to be familiar with the characteristics of the different fishing grounds, understand the tides on each, and also be proficient in the use of a sounding lead. He is responsible

[1] This [illegible] pearls. A trawler usually carries two or three sets of [illegible] sails [illegible] according to the strength of the wind [illegible] light winds [illegible] wind. As many different sizes of stay foresails and jibs [illegible] as circumstances demand, while the spare sails are stowed [illegible] below. Practically, of course, it is necessary to change [illegible] sails at night, and [illegible] important that the members of a smack's crew should be able to determine [illegible] what sail they put their hands on, since this knowledge obviates [illegible] work and delay.

Fishermen's Seamanship [illegible]

for all the ship's stores, which must be kept [illegible] use. He should have a thorough knowledge [illegible] horses [illegible] ship's [illegible] in the management of a vessel under [illegible] absence or [illegible] of the master, the mate must [illegible] charge of the ship and carry on the voyage.

The master [illegible] says Olsen, [illegible] to overlook the [illegible] and must [illegible] his [illegible] visions [illegible] voyage.

He must [illegible] see that every [illegible] and see [illegible] does his duty. He must [illegible] of his [illegible] He must [illegible] skillfully, know how to use the chart [illegible] soundings taken. He should [illegible] He must [illegible] bottoms and dangerous shoals [illegible] and [illegible] of the ground for fishing. He must [illegible] a good fisherman, so that he can manage his vessel [illegible] under all circumstances and pick a fare up [illegible] It is his duty to see that the vessel is properly secured [illegible] fishing [illegible] and [illegible] their places at [illegible] He [illegible] fish for market and arrange [illegible] He must see that the watches are properly kept [illegible] navigate the ship himself when going to [illegible] He must be ready at any moment [illegible] called, and use his superior knowledge [illegible] He must [illegible] his [illegible] keep his ship clean [illegible] always keep a good lookout.

The skipper and mate usually [illegible] crew and [illegible] and a part [illegible] members of the crew are hired.

[illegible]

Formerly the cook and third hand were apprenticed to the master or owner of a smack for a term of years, and when their apprenticeship expired they were promoted to higher grades. This system has been much modified if not abolished by recent acts of Parliament, one of which, the "Merchant Seamen (payment of wages and rating) Act," of 1880, it is alleged, had a bad effect on the crews, since it took away the control which the owners had previously possessed over their apprentices. It also combined with other causes to materially decrease the number of apprentices from Grimsby and Hull, and their places were filled by inexperienced boys taken from other trades, who frequently did not stay long enough on board the vessels to become serviceable and trustworthy. It has been put in evidence that—

In some cases the skippers and second hands were not so efficient as formerly, though it is said this was not the case; but the fear was generally expressed that this would steadily and rapidly increase as the existing men die out, and only men with inferior training are coming on to fill their places.

"The deep-sea fisherman's vocation appears to be a specialty, which requires time and special training to master, and one not easily taken up by the average seaman, however well trained in ordinary trades."

The fishermen employed in the British beam-trawl fishery are a hardy, robust class of men, and are distinguished for professional skill, bravery, and dogged perseverance, qualities which are such marked characteristics of seamen of the Anglo-Saxon race in all parts of the world. The majority of them are trained to the sea from childhood. A constant association with the perils and vicissitudes of a fisherman's life imbues them, even at an early age, with a sense of responsibility and fearlessness, qualifications which are necessary to their professional success. Then, too, the impressionable minds of the boys who constitute a portion of every trawler's crew soon become well stored with a knowledge of the details of fisherman's seamanship. Not only do the younger members of the crew learn the ordinary duties of a seaman, such as to "hand, reef, and steer," but they become familiar, as has been shown, with the construction and manipulation of fishery apparatus, acquire a knowledge of the different kinds of fish and their respective value, and later on secure important information relative to the fishing grounds and the seasons when fish are most abundant at special localities. All of this knowledge is, of course, of vital importance to the fisherman who aspires to success in his calling, and though the boy who begins his sea life at an early age may perhaps be deprived of many advantages that others may enjoy for obtaining a school education, it is, nevertheless, more likely that he will make a better and more successful fisherman than if he had more knowledge of books and less of his calling. Therefore, notwithstanding the system of apprenticeship which

Report of the Board of Trade on the system of deep-sea trawl fishing in the North Sea. London, 1883, p. 10.

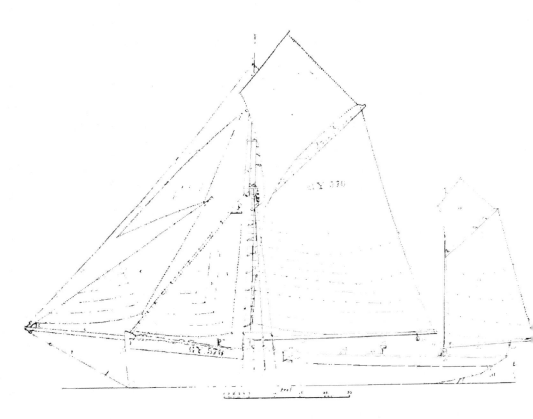

SAIL PLAN OF KETCH-RIGGED SAILING TRAWLER WILLIE AND ADA, OF GRIMSBY.

1. Jib-topsail
2. Jib.
3. Stay-foresail
4. Forward capstan
5. Tack ring or traveler.
6. Bowsprit.

7. Bobstay.
8. Main gaff-topsail.
9. Mainsail.
10. Main boom
11. Capstan
12. Trawl-warp roller

13. Dummy.
14. Cabin companion.
15. Stove pipe.
16. Mainsheet.
17. Mizzen stay.
18. Mizzen gaff-topsail

19. Mizzen or spanker.
20. Dandy winch
21. Spanker boom.
22. Spanker sheet.
a. Quarter line.
b. Parting line.

has been in vogue on the English trawlers may be open to many objections, it is nevertheless a fact that the training which boys get under such a system is important in producing a hardy, brave, and capable class of seamen, who are specially fitted for their vocation.

1. VESSELS.

The various types of vessels employed in the steam trawl fishery, namely, steam carriers, screw and side wheel steam trawlers, the North Sea sailing trawler, and the single-masted trawler, smack (also the smack's boat) have all been described very much in detail in the chapter on fishing vessels and fishing boats of Great Britain, to which reference is made for further information as to the construction, dimensions, and equipment of the British trawling fleet. Therefore to avoid a repetition of the details it is deemed necessary in this place to give only a general description of the various types of vessels alluded to above.[1]

The steam carriers, employed in transporting the catch of the trawling fleets to the more important markets—London, Grimsby, and Hull—are iron, ketch-rigged, screw steamers, designed especially for the trade. They have the reputation of being excellent sea-going vessels, and it is said that so well are the qualities of seaworthiness, capacity, and speed combined that though they are able to make headway against heavy head winds and seas, and to carry a large cargo, they nevertheless steam fast under ordinary conditions of wind and weather. Steam carriers were first introduced in 1864, previous to which time large sailing cutters were employed for carrying the fish from the trawling fleets to the markets.

The size varies somewhat, but the following dimensions of the screw steam carrier Lastralia, of Hull, one of the recent additions to the fleet, will give a fair idea of the proportions of the most approved type of these vessels. Length between perpendiculars 145 feet, beam 22 feet 6 inches, depth to top of floors 14 feet. (See Plate I, page 212.)

The steam trawlers are built of iron in some localities, but in other places, particularly in Scotland, wood is used in their construction. The majority are ketch or schooner rigged screw steamers, but a considerable number of side-wheel boats, chiefly tugs from the Tyne, are employed in trawling. The old Tyne tugs can not, in the true sense of the term, be called typical steam trawlers, since they were designed for other purposes, and have been used for trawling only because they failed to find employment in towing shipping—a result brought about by the employment of steam screw coasting vessels and a general decline in the towing trade from the Tyne. The steam trawler proper came

[1] At the time this paper was written the author expected to prepare a report on the fishing craft of the world, which it was expected would be published at the same time as this. The preparation of this report was abandoned after it had been partly completed.

into use about 1882, two vessels having been built and set to work in that year by the Grimsby and North Sea Steam Trawling Company, which has the reputation of being the first in England to construct vessels specially for this trade, at least the first to employ steamers successfully, though it is on record that experiments had previously been made to utilize steamers for beam trawling.

There is considerable variation in the size of the steamers employed in trawling. They range from about 40 to 120 tons. Among the largest are those from Grimsby, which generally act in the double capacity of catchers and carriers. The *Zodiac*, which was the pioneer vessel of the last mentioned class, is an iron ketch-rigged screw boat, 92 feet long between perpendiculars, 20 feet beam, 10 feet 6 inches depth of hold, and 192 indicated horse power. The *Grafton*, a Scotch-built schooner-rigged wooden screw steam trawler, one of the largest and finest of her class, is 108 feet long over all, 100 feet between perpendiculars, 19 feet beam, and 10 feet depth of hold. Her nominal horse power is 45, effective horse power 225. She steams 11 knots, and makes 11 knots under sail and steam.

A few side-wheel steamers have recently been built in Scotland specially for beam trawlers and for towing herring boats as well. Some of the fishermen report preferring this class of vessel to the screw steamers. These depend more entirely on steam power than the propellers, and therefore have only one mast stepped well forward, on which can be set a jib and mainsail.

As a rule, the screw steam trawlers are fine weatherly boats, and the best of them are probably not surpassed in sea-going qualities by any vessels in the world.

The North Sea sailing trawler is the most important type of vessel engaged in the beam-trawl fishery, if the numbers employed and the work it has to perform be taken into consideration.

With comparatively few exceptions these vessels are built of wood. A few iron smacks have been constructed, but they do not appear to receive much with general favor, judging from the fact that their numbers have not been materially increased of late years.

The North Sea trawler is designed to secure the maximum of sea-worthiness with a fair amount of speed. In the former quality it is probably not exceeded by any vessel of its size in the world, and although it is comparatively light rigged — jury-rigged — as it is called by some of the English fishermen — it nevertheless at certain times attains a moderately high rate of speed. It is ketch or dandy-rigged — the arrangement of spars and sails being specially well adapted to the work it has to perform. It ranges in size from 35 to 85 tons, though comparatively few vessels of this class are smaller than 50 tons, while many of those now being built range upwards of 70 tons. The following dimensions

See Report U. S. Fish Comm. for 1879, p. 38.
See Plate X, page 40.
See Pl. XI, p. 42.

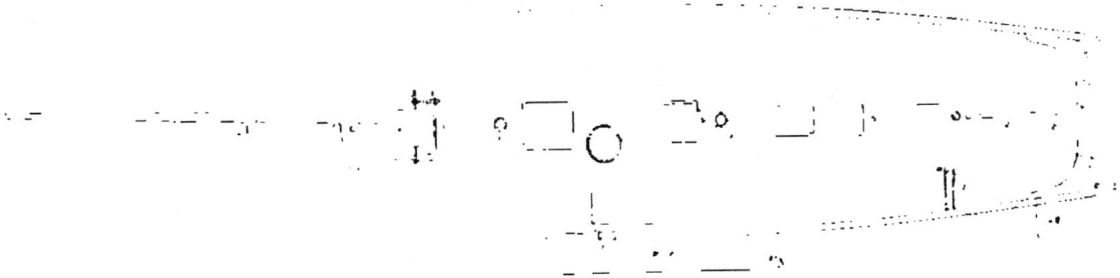

Deck Plan — William and Ada

of the smack *Willie and Edie* of Grimsby, in which the writer made a trip to the Dogger Bank, may be taken as a fair illustration of the proportions of the first-class North Sea trawler, though this vessel is not so deep as the majority of the class to which she belongs. Length over all outside of stem to outside of taffrail, 77 feet 6 inches; beam 20 feet, width of taffrail 12 feet; depth of hold 10 feet. 7 tons tons. The sail area would be from 700 to 740 running yards of 24-inch canvas; and the dimensions of spars is follows: Mainmast, deck to hounds 36 feet 4 inches, total above deck, 46 feet; main topmast, 35 feet; main boom 57 feet; main gaff 40 feet; main gaff topsail yard 17 feet; mizzenmast, above deck 37 feet; 10 feet of this above the cross of the mizzen cap-stile is tapered to form a pole topmast; mizzen boom 19 feet 6 inches; mizzen gaff 14 feet; mizzen gaff topsail yard 8 feet; bowsprit outside stem, 20 feet. (See Plates XII and XIII.)

Of late years many improvements have been made in the equipments of the sailing trawlers, among which the most important perhaps is the introduction of improved apparatus for heaving the trawl.

The next important type of trawling vessel is the single-masted smack or cutter employed chiefly in the south and west of England, from Wales, and also from Ireland. These vessels are much smaller than the ketch-rigged trawlers, and seldom exceed 50 tons in size. As a rule, they adopt the "single boating" system and it is necessary that they should be swifter than the vessels that follow the "fleeting." We therefore find that the Brixham smacks, which may be taken as the type of this class, are very sharp, deep, and rather narrow, with a proportionately large spread of canvas, the form and sail area being such as to insure a high rate of speed. At the same time they have the reputation of being fine sea boats, and there is probably not to be found in the fishing fleets of the world a higher combination of excellent sailing qualities and sea-worthiness than is possessed by some of the modern-built trawling cutters of the south of England. A builder's model of one of these vessels, that was exhibited at London 1883, represented the following proportions: Length 65 feet; beam 17 feet; depth 9 feet; draught of water from 10 to 11 feet.

We quote from Holdsworth the following notes on the history, rig, and general equipment of the vessels employed in trawling, which he wrote which may answer very well for the present time, with the exception that the introduction of steam trawlers from smacks, and a few other changes which have been noted, have occurred since his report was published.

"The vessels used for trawling are commonly called smacks. During the last twenty years great improvements have been made in their design with the object of making them faster, and in some few cases it may be a question whether by the adoption of very fine lines, sea-going qualities have not been to some extent sacrificed to the desire for increased speed. Formerly the smacks were much smaller than at the present time, and ranged from 25 to 36 tons N. M. They were built with the principal object of living through anything, and rarely failed to make good weather of it at all times. Many of these strong, well-built vessels are still at work, and would be likely to hold their own for many more years were it not that seagoing qualities are not the only ones required at the present day. Now the greater demand for fish and the increased number of smacks have led to more competition among the fishermen, and time has become more valuable, for the first boats in are able to get the best price for their fish. Most of the modern trawl vessels are of a large size, ranging up to 70 tons N. M., and are fine powerful craft of upwards of 60 feet keel and good beam. They are not as formerly built high at the bow and with plenty of sheer, making them easy and comfortable sea boats, and whilst their increased size enables them to use larger trawl beams and larger nets, the general improvement in our knowledge of shipbuilding has led to the adoption of finer lines in their construction, resulting in the much better sailing qualities which are now required to meet the demands of the trade. The speedy delivery of the fish is every day becoming a more important object as the demand for it increases all over the country, and the smacks may daily be seen racing back to the great trawling stations to land their fish, each one endeavoring, often with the help of balloon canvas, to bring her catch early to market, where the buyers are waiting with orders to purchase for all parts of the country.

The vessels regularly employed in trawling are, as we have said, called smacks, a term which appears to have been applied to fishing boats rigged as sloops or cutters. In these smacks the mast is stepped well forward so as to allow of a large and powerful mainsail, at the same time giving plenty of room for the stowage of a long trawl beam and large net when not at work. The rigging of these vessels was formerly arranged simply, and a long head to the mast to support the short topmast was all that was necessary when only a small topsail was to be set; but the large light sails now carried commonly require the addition of cross-trees and back stays to secure the spar under the strain it has to bear. In the west country the bowsprit is without any rigging, as the head sails are small, and it is desirable to have no bob-stay in the way of the trawl rope, which, being always hauled in over the bow, has to be led more or less outside clear of the rigging to one side or other of the vessel, according to which tack she is on when at work, and to be brought in accordingly on the gunwale amidships, where it is made fast to the pump-bitt. A large winch is fitted just before the mast for heaving in the trawl, and there is a small windlass astern, called the "dandy wink," stepped between the head of the companion and the bulwark.

[illegible]

[illegible]

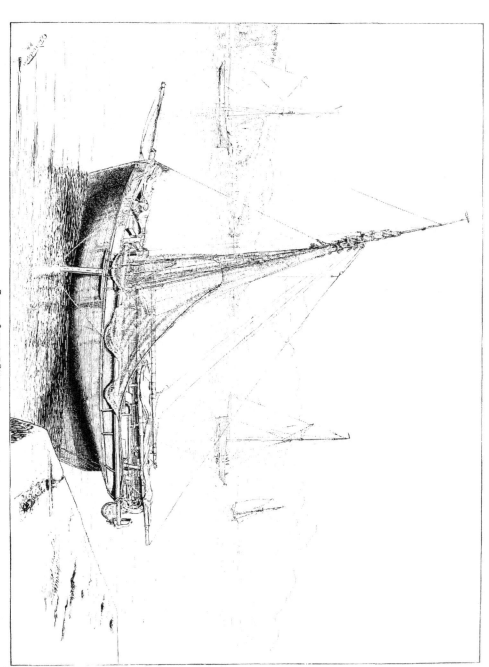

TRAWLING CUTTERS AT BRIXHAM.

Drawn by C. B. Hudson.

for hoisting up the after end of the beam when the trawl is got on board. In the North Sea trawlers the trawl warp is hove in and got in over the side by means of a patent capstan shipped near the center of the vessel. This excellent contrivance is worked by two ordinary winch handles, or by an arrangement of a wheel and pinion fitted either to the top of the spindle round which the capstan turns or to an iron standard by the side of the capstan.

"The large trawl vessels now in use from Grimsby and Hull, and recently built, are rigged in a different manner from that which has long been the general custom with the smaller craft. It was found that the increased size of the mainsail and heavy main boom necessary for these larger vessels required more hands to manage them, and as the quantity of fish taken by these vessels did not increase in proportion to the greater size—the nets used by them being only slightly enlarged—economy and convenience were both in favor of reducing the large mainsail if it could be done without seriously diminishing the working power of the vessel. The new trawlers were therefore built of considerable length, so as to give plenty of room for a good mizzenmast, the mast being stepped well forward to allow sufficient steering room aft; the large unmanageable mainsail was got rid of, and the reduction in its size made up by a good-sized mizzen. These vessels can now be worked economically, and the sails, being in comparatively small pieces, are managed with only one hand more than in much smaller craft. Although these large trawlers do not bring in much more fish than the vessels perhaps 15 or 20 tons smaller—as the longest beams now in use do not exceed 50 feet—it is believed their greater cost is compensated for by the additional accommodation provided. The crew have more room and increased cooking conveniences, and there is much better stowage for the ice and fish; and it speaks well both for the owners and the prosperity of the fishing trade that the men who are exposed to the hardships and dangers of the deep-sea fisheries are taken good care of by those who, having in most cases themselves gone through with the practical part of the work, are now in the happy position of owners, and can remain comfortably on shore.

"At Yarmouth, and some other places on the North Sea coast, the luggers, when not employed in herring fishing, are in some cases converted

[illegible] North Sea [illegible] the size of the [illegible] of the fishing grounds [illegible] little power [illegible] the large increase [illegible] fast-sailing cutters or steamers [illegible] smacks.

into trawlers, and as the lug rig is not very suitable for that mode of fishing a temporary change is made, and they are fitted out with a different set of masts and sails; the dandy, or perhaps speaking more correctly, the ketch rig with gaff sails being the one adopted, the same as just described in the large modern built trawlers at Grimsby and Hull. Some of the Ramsgate and Brixham vessels are now rigged in the same manner, and we have no doubt that it will be very generally adopted for the new vessels on various parts of the coast where deep-sea trawling is carried on, although as a rule fishermen are not fond of giving up what they have been long accustomed to. * * *

"In 1862 a new trawler ready for sea, and what was then considered one of the larger class, could be built and fitted out for £700 or £800; but the vessels before mentioned as having recently come into use at Hull and Grimsby can not be turned out ready for work for much less than £1,200 each. This includes a fit out of all that is required for fishing, and costs about £70 or £80. A fit out consists of a double set of almost every part of the gear, to provide against accidents, and generally to save the time which would be lost if the smack were obliged to return to port before she had done a fair quantity of work. A trawl net will perhaps last from two to four months, according to the nature of the ground worked on, but during that time parts of it will have to be renewed. The back of the net, being exposed to the least wear, lasts the longest; the under part will generally require renewing twice, and the cod five or six times before the net is finally condemned. The cost of a new net is about £9 when made of ordinary hemp, but manilla is coming into use for this purpose, as it is very much stronger, although more costly. It is dressed with coal tar, which preserves the material better than either Stockholm tar or tan. One of the large nets now used, and measuring about 50 feet across the square, can not be made for much less than £16.

"Barking the sails of fishing crafts is almost universal in this country. It consists in mopping them over with a solution of oak bark, tar, grease, and ochre, which acts as a good preservative to the canvas; this is done every six or eight weeks, and a yard is prepared and kept for the purpose at all the important fishing stations."[1]

II.—FISHING APPARATUS.

1. THE BEAM TRAWL.

The beam trawl has been described as "a triangular, flat, purse-shaped net, with the mouth extended by a horizontal wooden beam, which is raised a short distance from the ground by means of two iron supports or heads, the upper part of the mouth being fastened to the beam, and the under portion dragging on the ground as the net is towed over the bottom." The detailed description which follows refers more

[1] Deep Sea Fishing and Fishing Boats, pp. 69-70.

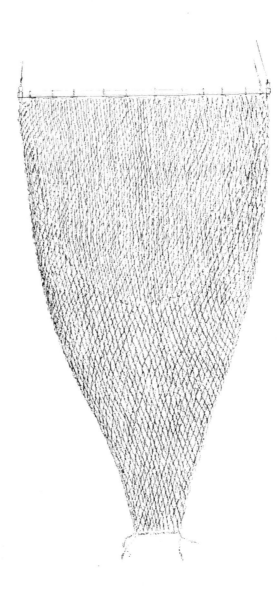

BEAM-TRAWL, FROM ABOVE, COD-END UNLOOSED.

particularly to the style of beam trawl used in the North Sea by the Hull and Grimsby fishermen, though it may be stated this has a close affinity to the trawls which are worked in the waters off Plymouth, Brixham, and other places in Great Britain.

(a) The Beam.

The beam is made of a length to correspond with the dimensions of the net, and the size of both the net and beam is usually adapted to the length and ability of the vessel which is to tow the trawl. The length of the trawl beams carried by the large vessels varies from 40 to upwards of 50 feet in length, though for inshore fishing the length is, of course, not so great, ranging anywhere from 10 or 12 feet upwards. The beam is usually made of ash, beech, or elm, the latter being preferred and most commonly used. Oak also is sometimes employed for this purpose, but is generally considered too heavy. For the larger beams it is sometimes necessary to use two or more pieces of timber, which are scarfed and banded with iron hoops, but a single stick, if easily obtained, is generally preferred. In either case the timber is selected as nearly the proper size as possible, and little more is done to it than to remove the bark from the stick and trim the ends so that they will fit into the sockets on the beam heads, where they are securely held by iron wedges driven around the wood. A piece of timber with a slight curve in it is generally preferred by the North Sea fishermen, this being so fitted to the trawl heads that the middle of the beam curves up and is somewhat farther from the bottom than the ends are. This is considered much better than a straight beam when fishing for haddock, hake, and other free-swimming fishes, but probably would have no advantage over the latter if sole, turbot, plaice, and other flat fish were the chief object of pursuit.

Holdsworth says: "The length of the beam for each vessel is mainly determined by the distance between the taffrail and the after shroud, convenience and security both making it desirable to carry the beam when not in use hoisted up alongside, with one end projecting just beyond the stern of the vessel, where it is made fast by a special rope or chain, and the other coming in front of the after shroud or shrouds. The advantage of this arrangement is obvious, as it is generally the case that the beam has to be hoisted up whilst the vessel is rolling and pitching about in a seaway. The after end of the beam is first got into place, and the fore part is then hoisted up until level with the top of the bulwark, over which and between two of the shrouds the iron head at the end of the

---

[1] [illegible] the best wood for the purpose, according to W[illegible] [illegible] possibly [illegible] day [illegible]

beam finds a snug berth, and all danger of the heavy and somewhat unmanageable spar swinging on board as the vessel lurches is avoided. It would be often difficult to prevent this if the beam were not long enough to overlap the after shrouds."[1]

The above statement applies more particularly to the single-masted cutters, but it may be said that on the larger ketch-rigged trawlers the forward end of the beam usually comes in abaft the main rigging, and is prevented from swinging across deck by a guy rope (one end of which is fast to the after main shrouds), which is taken around the head or the end of the beam by one man, who holds it firmly with a round turn on the rigging.

(b. The Trawl-heads.

The trawl heads, or head-irons, serve a variety of purposes, such as (1) weighting the trawl sufficiently to sink it; (2) supporting the beam, each end of which is firmly fixed at right angles into a socket, commonly called a "cap" or "joggle," above or below the top of the head-iron; (3) raising the upper part or back of the net, which is fastened to the beam, from the ground, thus keeping the mouth of the apparatus open sufficiently to permit the entrance of fish; (4) as a runner, which slides easily over the bottom, and to which are attached, on the front side, the towing bridles, while the foot rope and wings of the net are fastened to the rear of the trawl head.

There are several forms of head-irons used on different parts of the British coast, though those most commonly employed have a general resemblance to each other; local differences being due, in most cases, to some peculiarity which exists or has existed in the fishing from certain sections.

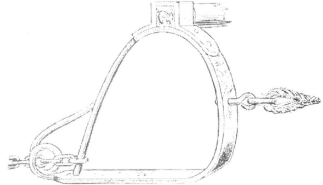

FIG. 1. TRAWL-HEAD.

From Grimsby, Hull, and other important fishing ports on the east coast of England a trawl-head like that shown in Fig. 1 is the prevailing

---

[1] Deep-Sea Fishing, etc., p. 55.

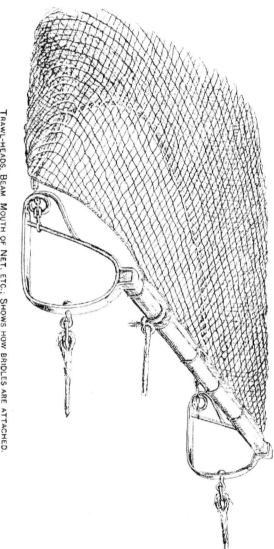

TRAWL-HEADS, BEAM MOUTH OF NET, ETC.; SHOWS HOW BRIDLES ARE ATTACHED.

pattern. The size and weight vary considerably, depending chiefly on the dimensions of the net, but also somewhat on the judgment of the skippers using them; some holding that a heavy head-iron is preferable, while others maintain that one of medium weight will fish as well and is easier to handle. On the larger class of North Sea sailing trawlers they range from about [illegible] to [illegible] pounds weight for the two heads.

Holdsworth says: "The weight of the two irons ranges in different parts of the coast from 2[illegible]0 to [illegible]0 pounds, and varies generally with the size of the net and, of course, as they do with the size of the vessel; but in some parts of the North Sea, where the tides are very strong, moderate-sized trawls require a great deal of weight in the head-irons to keep them on the ground. It is not to the interest of the fisherman, however, to weight his trawl beyond more than enough to keep his gear at the bottom under the ordinary conditions of working."

The trawl-heads of the smack *W[illegible] and [illegible]*, of Grimsby, 75.68 tons, weighed 180 pounds each; were 4 feet in length, 2 feet 10 inches wide in the broadest part, the iron of which they were made being 4 inches wide and three-fourths of an inch thick. The head-irons used on the cutter *Sobriety*, 75.29 tons, of the same port, each weighed [illegible]0 pounds.

As the North Sea trawlers catch large quantities of haddock, and more or less of other species of free-swimming fishes, it is desirable to have the beam farther from the ground than if flat-fishes were the only or chief object of pursuit; therefore the sockets into which the ends of the beam fit are placed on top of the trawl-head. Essentially the same form of head is used by the Brixham and Plymouth trawlers as that above described, these of course being somewhat lighter, as the vessels are generally smaller than those of the east-coast ports; while the heavy head-irons on the large vessels are perhaps generally lighter in proportion to their width than those commonly employed on the south coast. The trawl-heads are all made of wrought iron, the lower part—generally called the "sole" or the "shoe"—being of extra thickness, since this is exposed to the most wear as it slides over the bottom.

FIG. 2. BARKING PATTERN.

FIG. 3. TRAWL-HEAD, [illegible]

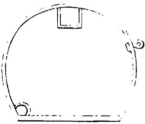

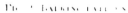

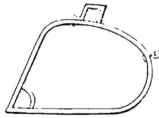

The peculiar stirrup-shaped head-iron (Fig. 2), known as the "Barking pattern," with its beam-socket beneath instead of above the upper port has been a long time in use by vessels belonging to the Thames. The statement has been made that it is now generally adopted by the Yarmouth smacks, having been introduced by the Barking vessels, many of which find it convenient to make that port their station.

The small trawlers which fish inshore in various parts of the British coast use another form of trawl head which is very much like that used by the Brixham men; the difference is that the iron hoop through which the ground rope passes before it is made fast is put inside instead of outside of the frame, as shown in Fig. 3.

Of late years several English inventors have brought out devices for improving the head irons. Perhaps the most noticeable of these is that invented by J. W. de Caux, Fig. 4, which was exhibited at London, and is constructed on the same principle as a Dutch pattern described in another paragraph. The trawl head of de Caux is wholly of iron, and consists of two strong iron plates arranged in a triangle, joined together at the apex so as to form a socket for the end of the beam, and each having a crutch or fork at its lower end that fits over a wheel, to the hub of which the extremities of the fork is fastened by a bolt, upon which the wheel when working revolves. The front wheel is a little

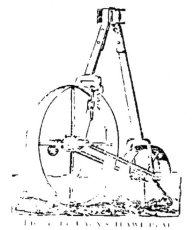

FIG. 4.—DE CAUX'S TRAWL BEAM.

more than double the diameter of the other; they are further connected by a stout iron bar which runs on either side from one wheel to the other, being fastened to the hub. A shackle and link for bending the trawl foot rope on is attached to the hub of the small wheel while a large shackle for the towing bridle is secured by a heavy bolt to the larger wheel. The wheels are broad iron bands with four spokes in the larger and three in the smaller one. The special advantages claimed for this apparatus are as follows: (1) It goes upon wheels which roll over and are not dragged through the ground. (2) The trawl beam can be carried at any height from the ground.

Though the advantages above named are perhaps important ones several trawl fishermen told the writer that they were opposed to using the Cox's device because, as they said, it is too liable to be broken in rough weather by slipping against the vessel's side, and it is not an easy matter to repair it at sea.

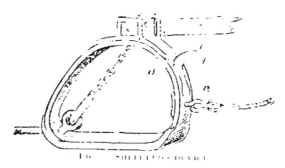

Fig. —SHEPHERD'S DEVICE.

H. C. W. Shepherd, of Lowestoft, exhibited at London a model of a beam trawl, to each head of which was attached a device—shown in Fig. 5—for ascertaining when the trawl is bottom up or the ground. It was explained to the writer by Mr. Shepherd that the tides between Holland and the English coast frequently run opposite ways, setting one way at the surface and in a different direction at the bottom. This peculiar action of the currents frequently causes the trawl which a vessel is towing to be capsized without, so far as the fishermen are able to tell by the surface water, there being any apparent reason for it. Therefore, according to Mr. Shepherd, much valuable time is often lost by the fishermen who, if using the ordinary form of trawl head, are not able to tell whether it is upset or not, the result being that they continue to tow it without, of course, catching any fish, and they do not learn the gear is inverted until it is hove up. The head of the trawl represented by the model above referred to would have the following measurements: Greatest diameter from lower after corner to center of front (outside to outside), 2½ feet, height, ground to top of head rail, 2½ feet, shoe on sole 6 inches by ½ inch iron, front 1½ inches by ¼ inch iron, eye to which bridle shackles 2 inches long, diameter of eye through which foot rope passes, 1½ inches. To the upper front side of the head is attached by the bolt d, a movable catch Λ, which has a stout slightly curved and pointed upper end. The lower part (when the trawl head is in its proper position) lies against the front of the head shoe, being longer and broader than the other, and at one point rounded, so that it will dig into the bottom like the fluke of an anchor. The purpose of

¹Mr. Sims writes in behalf of the committee: "There is no using the paper on trawling made by Mr. Ansted and he states no improvements in the shape of the trawl now for what of seventy years past, and the only difference is that it was extended in size."

the fish reaches the bottom over some point of the catch which is likely to be disturbed, strikes on the nose, and turns back, moving on the pond, and takes a sudden turn at a point in its head row. This movement causes the ground of a direction and act at right angles with the head row and is more readily adjusted, over the ground this point sinks into the bottom and either stops the progress of the vessel or causes the upper dress to have a sudden jerky motion, which indicates to the fisherman that the gear is exposed, he therefore proceeds at once to get it into proper position for fishing.

THE TRAWL NET

That portion of the apparatus to which the term trawl is more especially applied is the net. It is formed of several sections, each of which has a technical name, there being, however, local differences as to the terms applied.

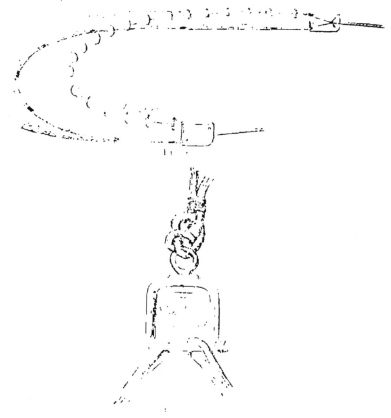

Here m the details as to whether a short, for instance, is the otter trawl has to understand which term one is referring.

Holdsworth [illegible] the [illegible] appliances [illegible] of its construction [illegible] cases it has [illegible] ations in shape [illegible] insuring the [illegible] enter whilst the net [illegible] at the bottom.

As has been [illegible] the upper part [illegible] part very much [illegible] perhaps [illegible] called the [illegible] is formed the [illegible] belly are composed [illegible] together to form [illegible] the square [illegible] belly [illegible] square is the front upper portion [illegible] and it is usually about [illegible] section called the [illegible] upper surface the front and is [illegible] on one side [illegible] The lower part of the [illegible] the square [illegible] in such a manner that the [illegible] extending from one trawl head to the other close [illegible] ground [illegible] the center of the curve of [illegible] some distance behind the beam and front of the net. The usual [illegible] curve is that the distance from the beam to the [illegible] the beam. In [illegible] however in all cases a considerable space [illegible] and back of the net must pass before [illegible] bottom are disturbed by the under part of the [illegible] beam about [illegible] feet [illegible] ground rope [illegible] portion [illegible] employed [illegible] there being [illegible] the [illegible] the Dogger Bank the [illegible] culty [illegible] fishermen [illegible]

We [illegible] catching soles [illegible] general fishing.

The portion [illegible]

[illegible]

the Fisheries [illegible]

"Each fisherman has his own fancy as to the fixing of the trawl in his own particular way in order to make more or less *bosom* to the trawl

" The narrow, straight sides of the net between the back and the ground rope, and extending from the trawl heads to nearly on a level with the bosom, are called the wings or gorings. they are generally made of separate pieces of net, and are inserted when the several parts composing the net are put together

The lower portion of the net immediately beneath the battings, and of similar size and shape, is called the belly or ground

"From the bosom the whole net, now forming a complete bag, tapers to the cod or purse, a length equal to about two-thirds of that of the beam. The cod is a narrow bag, about one-seventh of the entire length of the trawl. it is that part of the net into which all the fish which pass over the ground rope sooner or later find their way, and in which most of them are collected when the net is hauled in. The extremity or cod end is closed by the draw rope or cod line, which gathers the end of the net together and prevents the escape of the fish until it is got on board, when the rope is cast off, the cod end opened, and the fish fall out. The under part of the cod having a good deal of the weight of the fish on it, is of course exposed to a great deal of wear and tear as it is dragged over the ground; so to protect it from chafing and being destroyed, old pieces of net, termed 'rubbing pieces' or 'false bellies,' are fastened across it in such a manner as to overlap one another successively from one end of the cod to the other, and thus to relieve the strain on the net itself. * * *

Just above the entrance to the cod the pockets are placed one on each side of the interior of the main portion of the net. They are not separate parts of the net but are made by simply lacing together the back and belly for a length of about 16 feet in a line from the outer edge of the bag downwards and inwards to its small end and the commencement of the cod. This part of the bag is therefore divided into three spaces, and of nearly equal breadth at the lower end, those at the sides being the pockets, and the central space that through which the fish must pass on their way from the entrance of the net to the cod or general receptacle. This passage between the pockets is guarded by a veil of netting, called the 'flapper,' fastened to the upper part or back, and with its free edge directed towards the cod, so that the fish can easily make their way under it into that part of the net, but not so readily return. The mouths of the pockets face and open into the cod or end of the net where the fish are collected, and there being no means of escape for the fish at the cod end, many of them, and especially the soles, work their way along the sides of the cod into the pockets, continuing their progress in that direction till they are stopped by the

This is called the pokebine. By Crossley's sketch the term cod-line being applied to a piece of rope extending from the net-cod end of the beam to the cod-end

Diagram of Beam Trawl

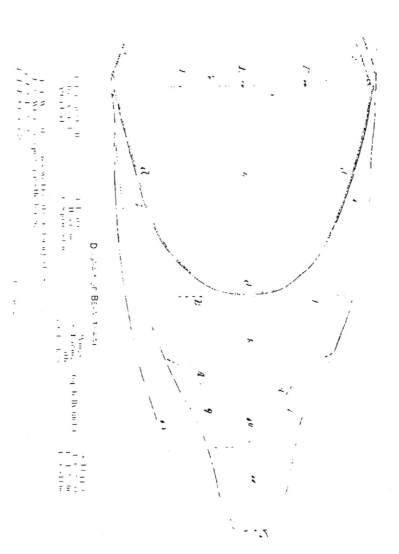

gradual narrowing, and termination of the bag found scraped on fastenings.

The several sections of the net having been joined together, the front edge of the square is hung to a ¾ to 1 inch iron rod called the head rope, which is fastened to the beam at each end, and generally in three other places at equal spaces on the beam. The end of the head rope that is on to the after end of the beam—that is the end of the beam which is nearest the trawl's own or vessel's—has a piece of chain 4 or 5 feet long attached to it; this is used to make fast it to trawl head, and chain is preferred since it is apt to be chafed by the dandy bridle. The "foot" of the net—that part which fastens to the foot rope—is first hung to a small metallic rope about 1¼ inches in circumference called the dolch line, which is a little longer; by the foot rope to which it is seized with marline, these being put on a foot apart on the wings and about half this distance on the bosom is the middle of the curve formed by the foot rope is called.

The foot rope is generally made of old towing hawser, which on the large smacks from Grimsby is about 7 inches in circumference. This is untwisted and laid up the opposite way, so that it will be more flexible. It is served or rounded from end to end with small rope six inches to 2½ inches thick being like the hawser partly worn. This rounding is put on for the double purpose of, 1, increasing the size of the foot rope, and thereby making it heavier, so that it will lie close to the bottom without being large, it is easier to drag along without digging into the ground and 2, for preventing the chafe to which it otherwise must be exposed.

The rounding is generally put on by machinery, since it is difficult to get it on properly by hand.

The trawlers that fish principally for soles generally put a piece of chain 15 to 20 feet long in the middle of the foot rope, or else weight it with lead, to make it sink into the ground, otherwise the soles would escape beneath it, as they lie so close to the bottom, often partly covered with sand or mud. When chain is used it is first wound round with old net until it is made as large as the rest of the foot rope when the whole is served with small stuff in the manner already described. To each end of the ground rope, and forming part of it, is attached a piece of chain which is long enough to fasten round the trawl head. In the trawling apparatus invented by de Caux the ground rope is fitted

FIG. —. NET WITH FOOT ROPE.

with rollers (Fig. —), which, it is claimed, facilitates its progress over the bottom.

Processed sheets of sole leather.

"The ends of the ground rope are made fast on each side by a few turns round the back of the trawl head just above the shoe, and the rope rests on the ground throughout the entire curve; the fish therefore, have no chance of escape at either the sides or bosom of the net, and their only outlet when once the beam has passed over them is in front, so that they must dart forward in the direction in which the net is moving to enable them to get clear of it. The object of making the ground rope of old material is that it may break in case of getting foul of rocks or any chance obstruction which may be met with on the generally smooth ground where a trawl can only be worked with advantage. If in such contingency the ground rope were strong and good the least mischief likely to ensue would be anchoring of the vessel by her trawl, involving great loss of time in clearing it, and resulting probably in breaking the beam, and other damage; but as these nets are used in deep water, where there is always more or less sea or swell the great danger to be feared when the net gets foul is the parting of the warp by which the trawl is towed, and the consequent loss of the whole gear. If however the ground rope give way the only damage likely to result is to the under part of the net behind it being torn open, the whole apparatus then comes away clear, when it can be hoisted up overhauled, and the netting and rope repaired. It was formerly the custom to weight the ground rope to insure its close working over the bottom, and it is still sometimes the practice at Yarmouth to use short lengths of chain for that purpose, secured at each end by rope yarns to the ground rope so as to be easily torn away in case of getting foul. The French trawlers also use chain on the ground rope, but in those we have examined a great length of chain has been suspended in short festoons and secured by iron rings over the rope, and therefore not easily detached. Our west country fishermen find that by giving a large sweep to the ground rope of old hawser it is heavy enough without other addition than the small rope with which it is covered or rounded."

The cod end of a trawl net, or at least such as are used on the large smacks from Grimsby, is made of double twine, and the meshes are smaller than in the other sections of the apparatus, which are made of single twine. Four sizes of meshes are used in the largest trawl nets, increasing from 1½ inches at the cod end to 4 inches in the back, while the underneath part of the net is generally made of twine a size larger than is used for the back.

The material used in the construction of the net is small, tolerably stiff about the size of marline, and essentially the same is the "lobster twine" that New England fishermen employ for a number of purposes. The nets are coated with coal tar.

A piece of old rope, six 2½ to 3 inches in size, called the "cod line" by the Grimsby fishermen, somewhat longer than the trawl and having

Increased at the cod end here.

The size of mesh of the trawl varies greatly, and is much smaller as we go south of Yarmouth. About Hastings the meshes diminish in some places down to 1 inches.

an eye splice in one end, is used to haul up the cod end when it is heavily weighted with fish, or when, as sometimes happens, it contains stones of considerable size. When either of these contingencies occur it is difficult, especially in rough weather, to pull the net over the smack's side with a heavy weight in the cod end dragging down. One end of the cod line is secured to the lower end of the net by the "poke line" with which the cod is tied up, while its other end makes fast to the forward trawl head.

(d) The Trawl Warp and Bridles.

The trawl is operated or towed over the bottom by what is called a "trawl warp" (A, in Fig. 9), usually a 6 to 7½ inch hemp or tarred manilla hawser 150 fathoms long, two strings of 75 fathoms each being spliced together to form it. One end of this, in which is an eye splice and thimble (E, Fig. 9), is shackled to two other pieces of smaller hawser, termed the "bridles" or "spans" (B, Fig. 9), each of which is 15 to 20 fathoms long. These lead one to either side of the trawl's mouth, where they are shackled to the swivel eye bolt in front of the trawl heads.

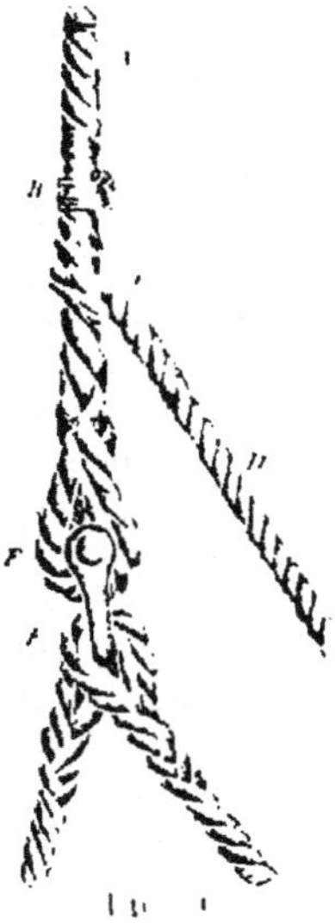

Fig. 9.

A smaller but somewhat longer rope, having a piece of chain at its lower end, is called the "dandy bridle" (D, Fig. 9). This is made fast permanently to that end of the beam which comes aft when it is taken on the rail, three or four turns of the chain on its end being taken around the beam; the extreme end is shackled to the trawl head or to the standing part of the bridle. The other end is secured to the trawl warp just above where the bridles shackle on, by a half hitch (C), with the end stopped back (b, Fig. 9).

The dandy bridle is used for convenience in heaving up and securing the after end of the beam to the stern of the vessel, its use preventing the necessity of rigging a derrick, as otherwise it is usually necessary to do. At present, however, the dandy bridle is quite generally adopted on the larger class of vessels.

(e) Dimensions and Method of Construction.

As a matter of interest in this connection I give detailed measurements of the trawls of two Grimsby smacks, the *Willie and Ada*, of 75.68 tons, and the *Sobriety*, of 75.29 tons.

The following are the dimensions of the trawl of the *Willa*

Length of beam [illegible]
Diameter of beam [illegible]
Weight of beam [illegible]
Height of [illegible]
Breadth across [illegible]
Weight of [illegible]
Thickness of [illegible]
Foot-rope [illegible]
Foot-rope [illegible]
Length of [illegible]
Size of rope [illegible]
Size of [illegible]
Length of [illegible] first [illegible]
Length of [illegible] from the foot [illegible]
Width [illegible]
Length [illegible]
Length of [illegible]
Length [illegible]
Width of [illegible]
Length of [illegible]
Size of [illegible]
Length of [illegible] of the net to [illegible] the length [illegible] the net [illegible]
Length of [illegible]
Length of [illegible]
Length of [illegible]
Length of [illegible]

The measurements of the trawl on board of the cutter Sc[illegible] pared very nearly with the above, the principal difference bei[illegible] foot-rope and weight of the heads, the height of the latter [illegible] same. The following will show the differences:

Length of beam [illegible]
Diameter of beam [illegible]
Length of foot-rope [illegible]
Length [illegible]
Weight of [illegible]

The following are additional details of the construction [illegible] ment of a beam trawl of the size mentioned above.

In making the net from 200 to 220 meshes are set up [illegible] of the square, and from 190 to 200 meshes at the bot[illegible] baitings or batings, which are joined to the square, are se[illegible] the same number of meshes as the bottom of the square, or 200, and are [illegible] down to 50 meshes, with 10 or 12 [illegible] added.

The ground or belly is made the same as the bating. The wings would be about 15 feet long. They would be

190 to 200 meshes [illegible] remaining meshes to [illegible] ends."

The "flapper" should [illegible] meshes at its end. [illegible] of the trawl net, and so [illegible] that it will drop down [illegible] apparatus is not moving [illegible]

Olsen gives the following [illegible] sections of a trawl net and [illegible]

"I would first count the meshes [illegible] upper part of the [illegible] correspond [illegible] Next I would count the meshes in [illegible] together; then I would stretch [illegible] end aft, and put the [illegible] fast to a spar lashed across the deck [illegible] and make them fast forward, then I [illegible] upwards. Now I would [illegible] lace from the head downwards.

"I would then take the [illegible] wings by finding the middle mesh [illegible] and clove hitch them on [illegible] little larger than the mesh. [illegible] deck and take the [illegible] measure it and tie the center meshes [illegible] the ground rope, set up taut with [illegible] ground rope up from the deck by placing a spar across the [illegible] Now I would measure the bosom and [illegible] square from quarter to head, allowing [illegible] the batch line, and complete the [illegible]

To put in the flapper and pockets he would [illegible] meshes under the back, lace the [illegible] 40 meshes, leaves 20 meshes on each side [illegible] lace up the pockets in a line with the flapper.

The lower part of the cod end [illegible] ers"—pieces of old net or some other [illegible] bottom of the trawl from being too quickly [illegible] the ground.

For rigging up the beam, [illegible] wedging the ends of the beam [illegible] 4 bridle thimbles, [illegible] 2 trawl warp shackles.

Various devices have been [illegible] tioned for improving the beam trawl [illegible] the purpose of allowing [illegible]

[illegible]

other advantages claimed by de Caux for improvements were the following:

1. Inside the trawl-net a smaller net is fixed so as to form a funnel to prevent the escape of large fishes.

2. The cod-end of the net is made so that when fishing the meshes are kept widely open to allow small fishes to escape therefrom.

3. At pleasure the net can be disconnected from the trawl-beam and the wheels at the bottom of the sea, and can be shut up and brought to the surface separately from them.

Whatever practical value these improvements have I am not prepared to say; the fact remains, however, that the common form of trawl is still almost exclusively in use. One inventor has an arrangement of frames, flat on the bottom and curved on top, over which the cod-end is drawn in such a way that the meshes are kept distended. Another proposes to accomplish the same result—namely; to allow the small fish to escape—by having a number of rubber grommets put here and there in the cod-end, these being sufficiently large to permit the small fry to pass through; and still another device consists in having the cod-end distended with larger hoops, the mesh much enlarged, and the lower part provided with an apron to prevent chafe on the bottom.

2. APPARATUS FOR OPERATING THE TRAWL.

In order that the manipulation of the beam-trawl may be more fully and clearly understood, it seems desirable that the various kinds of ap

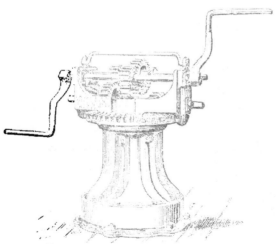

FIG. 10. AN EARLY TYPE OF CAPSTAN

paratus which have been devised especially for the purpose of handling it should be described in considerable detail. Though these form a portion of the vessel's equipment, and have been alluded to in a general way in that connection, still the various implements used in working a

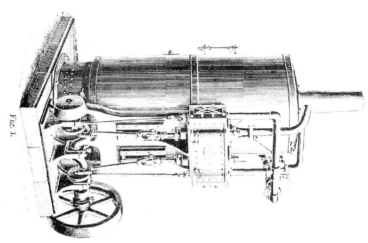

Fig. 1. Engine, front view.

BOILER AND ENGINE USED ON SAILING TRAWLERS.

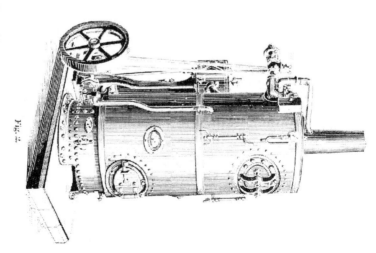

Fig. 2. Boiler, front view.

beam-trawl are almost as much a part of the apparatus as the trawl itself, and the successful prosecution of the fishery has, perhaps, been more dependent upon improved appliances for manipulating the gear than on anything else. The descriptions which follow are based chiefly on a study of the two Grimsby smacks upon which I sailed and which subsequent investigation has shown to be fair representatives of their class.

(d). The Capstan.

Several forms of hand-power capstans have been used for working the beam-trawl. The increase in the size of the vessels and fishing apparatus has not, as a rule, been followed by an increase in the number of men constituting a smack's crew, and as, of course, greater power is required to heave up the large trawls now in use, this has to be supplied by improved capstans, which are so constructed by a system of cog-wheels and ratchets (see Fig. 11), that as many as four different purchases can be obtained on some of them, the first being a very quick motion for pulling in slack warp; the fourth, a slow but most powerful one for a very heavy pull, while the others are intermediate; various degrees of power and quickness being thus combined in the same implement.

Fig. 11. AN IMPROVED CAPSTAN.

The necessity which exists for having increased facilities to raise the trawl from the bottom has led to the introduction, of late, of steam as a motive power for working the capstan, which is generally so made that it can be worked by hand as well, in case anything should make it impracticable to use steam. A vertical boiler and vertical engine are most commonly, if not exclusively, used, and the whole is made as simple as possible, in order that it may be managed by the fishermen with very little trouble. (See Plate XIII.) Steam capstans were first used on sailing trawlers in 1864, when the firm of Fowler & McCollin, of Hull, fitted one [illegible] This firm was succeeded by the Vulcan Iron Works Company, [illegible]. Each company, according to Mr. Charles Hellyer, [illegible] place, now manufacture the most approved [illegible] used in this kind. This arrangement consists of a [illegible] cylinders, each 4½ inches diameter [illegible] standard, independent of the [illegible] patent high-speed governor and throttle [illegible] force pump, etc. The boiler [illegible] cross tubes in the fire box, [illegible] and [illegible] and fittings, consisting of double [illegible] pressure gauge, [illegible] water gauges, blow-off cock, [illegible] consists of horizontal and vertical [illegible] bearing, friction clutch [illegible] spur pinion working into spur ring wheel [illegible] apparatus is so arranged that it can [illegible] by means of a lever on deck or in [illegible].

Mr. [illegible] gives the following additional particulars in [illegible], July 27, 1883, concerning the use of steam on [illegible]:

[illegible] most vessels of this kind for the purpose of [illegible] in modern times. The machinery on [illegible] vertical boiler and a pair of inverted [illegible] engines. The boilers generally used for this purpose [illegible] inches to 4 feet in diameter and 6½ to 7½ feet [illegible] cross tubes, all parts having to be [illegible] for frequently the attendance is not [illegible] although some smacks carry a proper [illegible]. The diameter of the cylinders is 5 to [illegible] 10 to 12 inches, the steam pressure [illegible] pounds. The price of such an engine and [illegible] of water tank, is from £125 to £145. [illegible] tank for fresh water holding 800 to 1,200 [illegible] Mr. [illegible] an unnecessary refinement. Probably [illegible] and careful engineer on board, who [illegible], and considering the simple nature of the [illegible] would answer very well for feed, and the room that [illegible] water tanks could be better utilized.

[illegible] Decks, Windlass, Wind[illegible]

[illegible] described [illegible] as being shipped between [illegible] and the bulwark, and this description [illegible] applies [illegible] to the Plymouth and Brixham trawlers [illegible].

[illegible] is placed some 10 or 12 feet aft

[illegible] International Fisheries Exhibition, [illegible]

PLATE XIV.

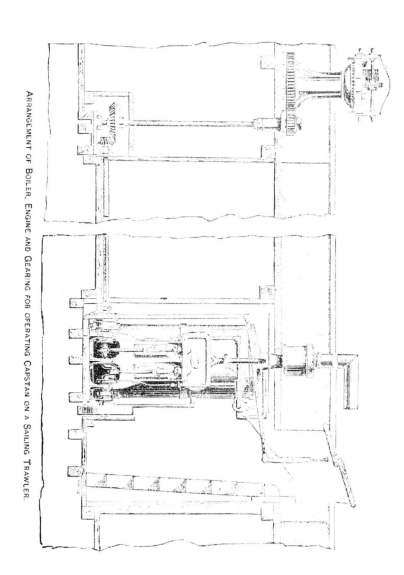

ARRANGEMENT OF BOILER, ENGINE AND GEARING FOR OPERATING CAPSTAN ON A SAILING TRAWLER.

of the companion, and generally almost directly abreast of the mizzen mast. A strong bitthead firmly secured to the deck leads of on the after side—similar in shape to and answering the same—serves as support for one end of the dandy wink, and the gearing by which it worked while an iron spindle in the opposite end is seated close to the rail, to which is also secured a dog or pawl which dropping into an iron ratchet on the end of the wink prevents the latter from turning back. (See Fig. 12.) The arrangement of cog wheel work on this is

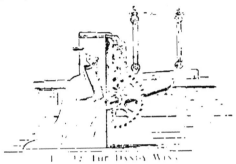

FIG. 12. THE DANDY WINK.

is such that two purchases can be obtained, one giving a rapid motion to the barrel of the winch, and the other but more powerful purchase turning it slower. It has already been explained that these men heave up the after end of the beam by means of the dandy wink.

c. The Forward Winch

Another winch, which is used in handling the trawl stands about half way between the windlass and mizzenmast on the larger ketch-rigged trawlers. This is worked like the others with a crank—one on each end if necessary. It is supported by two bits which are from 3 to 4 feet high. On the starboard end is a large cog wheel into which a smaller cog wheel on a shaft that is seated to the forward side the bits. If only a small power is required the wheels are uncoupled and the crank shipped on the shaft to which the power is to be applied.

d. The Dummy

Some 4 or 5 feet forward of the companion and almost exactly in center of the deck—either way—stands a large round post some 2 feet high called the dummy. (See Fig. 13.) This has four or more wheels on it, and the trawl warp is secured round it when the trawl is being shot, and to this stanchion too the warp is fastened while the gear is out and being towed over the ground.

e. The Trawl Warp Roller

Fixed between two stanchions, on the port side of and just forward directly abreast of the capstan is a large iron roller. (See Fig. 14.) for trawl warp to pass over when it is being hove in. This iron core which ratchets on the forward end, into which a pawl falls to prevent its turning back.

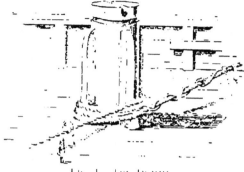

Fig. 1.—The Dummy.

The trawl roller of a vessel of 50 to 75 tons will be 144 inches long, 11 inches diameter at the ends, 7 inches diameter in the center. The roll is fixed so that it will turn back on a hinge, and a piece of bulwark is made to fit in snugly over the roller when it is not in use, but is, of course, removed whenever the trawl warp is hove in. (See Fig. 15.)

Fig. 14.—Frame Warp Roller.    Fig. 15.—Roller in Use.

On the single-masted trawlers of Brixham and Plymouth the trawl warp roller, which is much shorter, is placed on the port side of the stem head.

Dandy Bridle Chock.

Fig. 16.

A large iron chock, with a roller fitted into it (see Fig. 16), is secured to the port side of the taffrail. When the after end of the trawl is being hove up, the dandy bridle is taken across through the chock and thence to the dandy winch.

(b) Fish tackle.

A heavy purchase tackle is used for hoisting in the cod end of the trawl. The upper block of this tackle is usually threefold, and hooks somewhere about the mainmast head or beneath the crosstrees. The lower block is double or treble. The fall is 2 to 2½ inch manila rope. When the lower block has been hooked into the strop which is put around the cod end, the end of the fish-tackle fall is usually rove through a snatch block hooked near the foot of the mainmast, and taken thence to the forward winch.

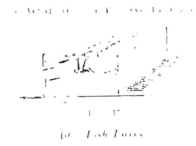

[illegible]

FIG. 17.

(c) Fish boxes.

All of the trawlers which fish in fleets in the North Sea use oblong wooden boxes, generally called "trunks" (see fig. 17), to pack their fish in. These are of uniform size and hold from 80 to 90 pounds of fish, the difference in weight depending chiefly on the kind of fish; some species of flat fish—the sole, for instance—pack very closely, and consequently weigh more than a box of haddock or cod. The boxes are partly covered by a strip of board nailed on each side of the top, while an oblong hole, large enough for a man to get his hand in, is cut near the upper edge of each end. In handling the boxes after they are filled these holes are very convenient, as they afford a hand hold, and they are also of service for reeving through the lines and [illegible] from end to end of the box to hold the fish in position.

The Brixham trawlers, who carry their fish to market every day, or perhaps twice a day, use small baskets called "pads" and "half pads."

Holdsworth says: "The packages in which the trawl fish are stored have lost much of their significance as denoting any particular capacity. Pads and half pads were once recognized measures, and are still spoken of in some of the markets, although the quantity of fish contained in them is rather uncertain. Ten years ago (about 1864) they were the only packages used by the Hull and Grimsby trawlers. The pad consisted of three 'pots,' and the half pad of two pots of fish. This division of a package into three or two imaginary parts called 'pots' was for the convenience of the salesmen and buyers; for instance, if two pads and three half pads were to be sold, they were offered as twelve

pots, fish were used to be worth so much per pot one day, and so much another day. This measurement was also found very convenient by the fishermen in case they had not enough prime fish at the end of their packing to fill a half pot; they still put it into a half-pot basket and called it a pot. At one time pot baskets were used, but they have been long given up. Formerly speculative dealers used to bargain with some of the fishermen to take all their prime fish at so much per pot, and then a pot was to weigh 40 pounds; but a half pot (two pots) subsequently came to weigh from 80 to 120 pounds, the difference being caused by the fish being more or less piled up on the top of the basket. A further change was made by the introduction of wooden boxes called trunks, and they were used especially for the package of soles; a trunk or box of soles usually containing from sixty to seventy pairs, weighing about 100 pounds. Plaice and haddocks are also packed in them, about forty of the latter, when sold for the fresh market, going to the box.

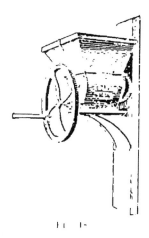

Fig. 4.

Ice Mill.

Most of the North Sea trawling vessels, especially those which go single-boating, carry a portion of the sea, carry an ice mill which is used for grinding up the ice that the fish are packed in. This mill is generally secured to a bulkhead in the ice house below deck. It has three revolving barrels fitted with strong steel teeth, and is operated by a crank wheel which, by a system of connecting cog wheels, causes the

The use of a wooden receptacle for the sea fish, called the "trunk," as a package for soles and plaice in the sea market is probably due to the ease of stowage, since the boxes are more readily handled and stowed than baskets could be, and are therefore safer.

barrels inside to turn in such a way that the ice is broken or picked up fine enough for use.

c . Boats.

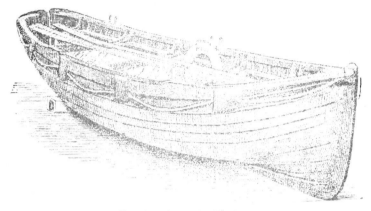

FIG. 19.—A TRAWLER'S BOAT.

The boat (see Fig. 19) used on the trawlers for transporting the fish from the catcher to the carrier is an open, clinker built, keel craft, wide, and rather clumsy looking, with full rounding bow and heavy square stern. It is strongly built, and has a large carrying capacity. The boats carried on the larger trawlers are about 17 feet long, 6½ to 7 feet wide, and 2 feet 9 inches deep.

The dangerous work performed by these boats is detailed elsewhere, but it may be said here that, because they are frequently capsized and the men in them drowned, an effort has been made to provide them with some kind of suitable appliance which may render them unsinkable and insure the greater safety of their crews. Many devices for attaining this much-desired end were shown at the London Fisheries Exhibition, in 1883, but none of them met with the full approval of the examining jury.

(d). Doddle Net or Diddle Net.

A dip-net, called a "doddle" or "diddle" net, forms part of the equipment of a trawler, and is used to dip fish out of the trawl when an unusually large catch has been made and the weight of fish in the net is too heavy to hoist in. At such times a hole is cut in the back of the trawl and enough fish removed with the dip-net to lighten it ; on some extraordinary occasion perhaps two or more holes have to be made in the net. The doddle net resembles the dip-net used by the New England mackerel seiners, though it is not quite so large as the latter.

6. METHODS OF FISHING.

GENERAL DESCRIPTION OF THE USE OF A BEAM TRAWL.

To obtain the greatest success in trawling one condition is especially desirable—that of having a moderately strong and favorable tide, since the trawl is always towed as nearly as practicable with the set of the current, but somewhat faster, as it will then work to the best advantage, being easily kept on the bottom over which it passes steadily. This is necessary, for the net being lighter than the beam clouded as the latter is with the iron heads, would otherwise be liable to drift forwards and thus prevent the entrance of fish. A moderate excess of speed in the trawl over the tide, varying according to the strength of the wind from half a knot to about a knot and a half per hour, keeps the net expanded and in a proper position on the bottom, so that the best results can be secured.

It is perhaps most desirable to have the tide setting nearly at right angles to the wind, since then the trawl can be towed equally well on either tack, as the set of the current changes with the ebb or flood. As, however, the tide is run is frequently to leeward or to windward, or is in any other way, much care and skill is necessary to work the trawl to the best advantage, so that it will keep the ground, will pass over the bottom as fast as is necessary, and also not be upset. It may be explained here that with a weather tide, the vessel is, or should be, put on whichever tack will permit her to tow the trawl as nearly as possible in the direction the current is going, and the best authorities say the warp should be kept well off. If working with a lee tide considerable care is necessary to prevent the vessel from broaching-to, so that she will run the tide, in which event she would be likely to upset the trawl.

"When a vessel has arrived on her fishing ground," according to Holdsworth, "the best part of the tide is chosen for beginning work, as she can then tow for several hours in the same direction, and the usual practice is to keep the trawl down till the tide is done—about five or six hours."

This is doubtless correct in a general sense, but in these days of sharp competition there are probably few skippers who will not put out their gear at half tide if they have reached a favorite fishing ground and the conditions are favorable for trawling.

When the ground is reached the vessel's head is laid in the direction in which it is going to tow—this, as has been explained, depending on the direction of the current; but whether on the port or starboard tack, she lays up by the wind, or nearly so, six within 5 or 6 points, at least until the trawl is set. After the trawl is out she may be kept off nearly before the wind, but as a rule, especially with moderate breezes, the vessel's course is laid nearly at right angles to the wind, so that it

TOWING A BEAM-TRAWL.

may exert its fullest force on the sails. If the [illegible] is [illegible] all is kept on the vessel [illegible] [illegible] duced so that the smack will go along [illegible] ing or heeling over.

* What the trawlers like [illegible] Holds [illegible] breeze—one that would enable them to do [illegible] knots off the [illegible] when the trawl is not overboard. They can then afford to lose [illegible] knots by the resistance of the net [illegible] it to do its work properly. Winter is the [illegible] then there is pretty sure to be plenty of wind [illegible] always be reduced; but unfortunately strong wind [illegible] by a good deal of sea, and when that is the case [illegible] of extra warp is allowed [illegible] jerking, it is difficult [illegible] There is always danger [illegible] certainty of doing so, and of losing the whole [illegible] then get foul, and besides this the difficulty of heaving up the [illegible] is greatly increased. Two or three nets are often spoiled [illegible] and the fish are liable to be killed and [illegible] they can be got on board. All of these circumstances [illegible] duce the fishermen to wait for more moderate [illegible] only a day or two or perhaps more; but in any case the supply [illegible] sent to market is lessened, for the same weather which puts [illegible] to the work of one vessel having probably the same effect on [illegible] those fishing in the same district. The Plymouth [illegible] tally subject to loss of time from bad weather in winter [illegible] son southwesterly winds prevail at the mouth of the channel, and [illegible] is commonly a good deal of sea setting in over the very limited [illegible] ground, only a few miles from the land. Although [illegible] work when it blows very fresh, a succession of [illegible] a stop to trawling there, and the supply of fish landed at Plymouth fluctuates more than on any other part of the coast.

SETTING A TRAWL [illegible]

If a vessel has just arrived on the ground and the bridles are first [illegible] up from the hold—where they are stowed with the [illegible] not in use*—and shackled to the trawl heads, and then coiled on deck, the fore bridle forward and the after bridle just before [illegible] dandy winch. The end of the towing warp is then taken up [illegible] three turns are thrown around the dummy [illegible] of the warp being on top—and then the bridles are shackled to [illegible] their coils arranged to run clear. The dandy bridle is next [illegible] which the end passed outside the mizzen rigging and sent to the [illegible] hawser, just above where the other bridles are shackled on [illegible]

* When the vessel is on the ground [illegible] fishing, the bridles are rarely [illegible]

close hatch, the end being stopped back with a small rope. In the mean time (or previously) the cod end is tied up with the cod-poke line, one end of which is taken through the eye splice in the lower end of the long cod line, which reaches to the beam. The trawl is now all ready to be shot, and the beam lies stretched along the port side of the vessel resting on or against the rail from the taffrail nearly to the main rigging, with the net piled loosely over it, the forward trawl head resting on deck and held in place by a stopper, while the after trawl head, which is outside the stern, is held by two short ropes called scanting lines, and which serve the several purposes of supporting the after end of the trawl when the dandy bridle has been slackened off, scanting and holding firmly in place the trawl head, and also for cutting the apparatus when it is being shot.

All hands are required to shoot a trawl.

"On the port tack," writes Olsen, "the captain on the quarter deck gives his orders, looses to see the trawl all clear, over the side, attends the after stopper, and squares the gear. The mate and third hand unlashes, stretches the trawl, and clears nails over the gear away. The fourth hand stands by to let go the tow head, and the cook takes the helm."

The following are the details of shooting a trawl as observed by the writer:

When all are ready, the lashing is taken off the forward trawl head, the captain casts on the scanting lines and holds them in his hands with a single turn round a belaying stern timber. The cod is now thrown out followed by the rest of the net until the whole is clear of the side and trailing out from the beam, which still remains in its place. The time having now arrived the trawl is lowered, and considerable skill is required to do this properly, for simple though it may seem, much care must be exercised to ensure the landing of the net and beam on the bottom in the right position, namely: With the ground rope below, and the beam upwards resting on the trawl heads, the mouth of the upper thus being distended. Unless the lowering is skillfully performed the trawl may strike the bottom on its back, which would result in its mouth being closed, therefore no fish could be taken. After the forward head and end of the beam are thrown out the captain slacks away a little on the scanting lines until the after end of the beam is nearly to the water but he does not let good them and the forward end of the beam swings off from the vessel's side, it at an angle of about forty-five degrees being slacked away gradually by one scanting bridle. When the beam is two or three fathoms astern of the smack the tow bridle and dandy bridle are usually checked in order that the skipper may see that the trawl is all right. As soon as the bridles are out the gear is again stopped from running to ascertain if the bridles lead clear, and a good pull is given the vessel so that she may start ahead and straighten the trawl. One

Fisheries of Sweden, p. ___.

According to Holdsworth ___ the dandy bridle to the tow end, whereby ___ trawl could have [illegible] is stationed at the [illegible] rope is around the [illegible] warp [illegible] ter being controlled by [illegible] orders. When 20 fathoms of [illegible] checked, and this is [illegible] every [illegible] hawser and pull the [illegible] amount of warp [illegible] by the skipper, who [illegible] ous conditions of [illegible] that are sought. [illegible] down, which would [illegible] the vessel moved [illegible] then floated in the water [illegible] of "slack" whether [illegible] It sometimes happens [illegible] most precautions [illegible]. When this happens the [illegible] of the warps as the [illegible] wrong, and, of course [illegible] shoot it properly.

If, however, the gear is [illegible] shooting [illegible] back again if the trawl has not sunk too far.

"To do this," writes Olsen [illegible] the [illegible] take the dandy [illegible] over the [illegible] it, and cast the gear back again."

If the trawl seems to be working [illegible] made fast with [illegible] trawl rope stopper [illegible] 5 fathoms long, the bight of which is secured to [illegible] lower part of the dummy. The ends of this [illegible] the trawl warp in opposite directions over and [illegible] overlap at each turn, which [illegible] stopper, and one end is fastened to the [illegible] called a [illegible] (See fig. [illegible], page [illegible].) When this is [illegible] stopper behind the dummy is cast off [illegible] slackened up—sometimes [illegible] that the strain all comes on the stopper. The purpose of [illegible] to save the warp [illegible]

[illegible] is very [illegible] the [illegible] vessel [illegible] The [illegible] from the vessel [illegible] the stopper [illegible] worked. This rope is [illegible] brought [illegible] should fall [illegible] now held by the [illegible] hangs [illegible] gear on the vessel and [illegible] warp [illegible] ton, which, as the vessel [illegible] small rope, and generally one considerably worn, it would under any sudden strain break before the hawser, and the trawl would not be lost. When this happens, more warp is paid out, and the vessel is started in a direction which may perhaps clear the obstruction. If this is not accomplished, the next thing to be done is to try and heave up the apparatus. As the warp becomes nearly perpendicular and the strain increases, the trawl generally comes away clear, frequently with only the net damaged, though the fishermen are not always so fortunate.

In winter a hawser is used instead of a trawl rope stopper. This device is made of a piece of old towing hawser that is not good enough for towing. It is 15 or 20 feet long, with an eye splice at each end, and well parceled to prevent it from chafing on the rail. The inner end is shackled to a chain cable on the dummy, and the other is fastened in the usual manner to the towing hawser, and reaches just outside the rail. The hawser is used to save the towing rope from chafing on the rail. When towing a trawl with strong winds, the warp is taken off the dummy and the bight carried forward and stoppered to the fore stay with a good piece of rope, and turns are put on the capstan ready for heaving. The bight is also supported along the rail with rope yarn. These precautions are taken to clear any vessel that may be seen to leeward by coming in stays, which the smack will do at once if the stopper holding the hawser is cast off. They are also necessary to prevent the loss of the trawl when the latter comes afoul of rough ground or any object on the bottom, such as a wreck, anchor, etc. The hawser will part under a sudden heavy strain, and is, or can of course, be cut if it can not be otherwise cleared soon enough; the vessel then swings at once head to the wind.

After being stopped the trawl rope is parceled where it comes across the rail; it is then pushed into the proper place, where it is held by stout hard wood pins which are stuck in holes bored in the rail. It may be explained here that on top of the main rail is fastened a false rail 4 inches thick, to take the scuffing of the towing hawser, and through both of these rails are bored 1½-inch holes 18 inches apart near the after end, where the warp usually comes, and 24 feet apart further forward. The position of the trawl warp on the rail depends on how the captain wants to keep the vessel's head. If for any reason it is desirable to keep her nearly before the wind the warp is shoved aft to the mizzen rigging, while if she lies still too broad the hawser is put further forward and a pin stuck in the rail ahead of it. Sometimes it is necessary to take the warp to the capstan, which is several feet forward of the dummy, but generally the vessel will lay near enough the wind without doing this.

When the trawl is out the tiller is allowed to swing, the sheets are eased off a little, and, as a rule, the towing hawser is placed so that the smack will head a point or two off the wind. The amount of sail set when towing the gear, as has been stated, depends on the strength of the wind. The trawlers are all provided with large light sails for use in moderate weather, as well as a large mizzen staysail or the latter sheeting well aft of the mainmast, and having the special name of "towing foresail."

It will readily be understood that the resistance offered by the trawl materially decreases the speed of the vessel. A smack that is running along from 8 to 9 knots will not tow her trawl faster than 1½ to 2 knots, which is considered fast enough; as now, if the gear is pulled along too rapidly it will not keep on the bottom.

SHOOTING A TRAWL FROM A STARBOARD SIDE — SMACK SHOOTS ACROSS THE STERN.

It has already been explained that the trawl, when up, is always carried on the port side, and is also hove up there; therefore it will be obvious that when it is put out from a vessel with her starboard tacks aboard, it must be shot round the stern. To do this, first supposing the bridles are shackled on the trawl heads, and the cod end tied up, the after bridle is passed round the stern and coiled down, the end being taken forward of the starboard mizzen rigging. The dandy bridle is next taken round the stern under the after bridle, hauled taut and made fast to coil amidships, after which it is coiled down ready for running. The bight of the fore bridle is made fast at the port mizzen rigging with a slip-stopper, and the end taken round outside of all and in forward of the starboard mizzen rigging. The end of the trawl warp is next taken around to stern outside, and in to all the bridles and brought in amidships on the starboard side, where it is pulled over to take turns round the dummy, the bridles are then shackled on, and the end of the dandy bridle made fast. When all is ready, and the vessel going through the water for 4 knots, the captain orders the men to pay out the net, and at the same time gets the "quarter strap" and cutting line all ready to slip, but holds on to them until the forward end of the beam swings clear of the smack's side as previously described. As he slacks away, the dandy bridle leading from the starboard side, and the fore bridle from the port quarter take the strain and the trawl shoots round or across the stern nearly at right angles with the vessel's keel. When the beam is square, the dandy bridle and fore bridle are shackled away, and the trawl warp paid out and stoppered in the same way as if the vessel was on the port tack.

Sometimes the dandy bridle is passed round the stern with the fore bridle over all of the vessel's bottom. In this case the bridle is coiled down round the stern to the starboard side of all to prevent others over the cod end of the warp and the process of making fast to the trawl warp. The bight of the bridle being passed and coiled down beneath the keel so that the warp is pulled clear, and as the vessel from the port to the starboard side. And the mizzen rope is let away from the process. As however, the hawser could not haul clear unless there was clear and at that post, one except in smooth water. A vessel, therefore is shot from or hove, as bight being stopped if necessary, after the trawl warp is being towed during.

As a rule, when the trawl is out on the starboard tack, a guy is set from the bow to the towing warp and securely fastened, or may be a bight of the hawser itself is taken up around the bow. This is a necessary precaution at night or in thick or rough weather, since she may then be ready to tack ship either to clear another vessel or to heave to in a gale. If necessary the trawl stopper is cast off, the jib sheet slacked, the helm put down, and though she may have little way the vessel works quickly, the towing warp pulling at her bow materially assisting her in stays.

After the trawl is down, if it is during the day and reasonably good weather, the fourth hand—usually a lad of sixteen to eighteen years of age—keeps the watch, takes notice how the trawl is working, and looks out for signals from the admiral if fishing in a fleet. If fishing at night the watches are kept by the second and third hands. It is a part of the duty of the watch to trim the sails, if necessary, and to keep as much in the wind as well as to observe how the trawl is working. By tending the warp outside the rail one can easily tell whether the trawl is working right or not. A jerky irregular motion is thought, the trawl constantly being caught on something, shows that it does not draw steadily on the bottom or is evidence that it is going over rough ground or possibly that it has capsized. If however the vibration is regular and comparatively slight the experienced fisherman knows at once that the apparatus is going all right.

According to Mr. Hellyer, the best way to tell whether a trawl is set or not is to put the ear down to the warp outside of the rail, though as stated above, an experienced trawler will generally be able to tell whether his gear is fishing or not by putting his hand on the warp.

14. CHANGING THE TACK WITH A TRAWL DOWN

It often happens, especially when fishing at night, that owing to change of tide or because a vessel may have reached the limit of suitable ground, she is obliged to change her tack if possible without setting her trawl, since in the latter case the gear would have to be hove up or else no fish would be taken. Of course the gear could be hove at the start, but this would cause the loss of much valuable time, perhaps two hours or more of good fishing, besides the crew would be forced to do extra labor, and also have their night's rest broken.

(a) To wear the trawl around.

When the tide is swinging around by the lee, or when the wind is moderate, it is generally found the safest, in order to prevent the gear from upsetting, *to wear the trawl around*. This is done as follows: towing on the starboard tack, with a moderate breeze of wind the bight of the trawl warp is stoppered near the stern with a stout piece of rope,

---

¹ Little day fishing is done except in summer and at best season the majority of the North Sea vessels, at least fish in fleets.

the stopper at the dummy is cast on the bight of the hawser hove over the rail, and the slack of it is pulled in on to port side. In the mean time the foresail is hauled to windward and the boom put hard up and the after sheets eased off a little. As the vessel falls off she comes quickly down, and is about to gybe, the trawl warp is stoppered at the dummy on the port side, and the fast on the starboard quarter is cast off. This generally has the effect of easing the strain to some still more, the wind luffily catches the sails on the port side, when the vessel comes to at once, so that she heads, as it is intended she should for towing.

In wearing from the port to the starboard tack, the only difference is that the bight of the trawl warp must be passed round the stern, and generally after this is done a new turn of it to heave over the dummy. Ordinarily a handy smack will wear the trawl round without difficulty, but in light winds it often takes some time to perform this evolution. This manœuvre is described as I saw it performed on the *Willie and Ada*. Some fishermen have a slightly different method I believe. They prefer to take a guy from the lee side round the stern, which they make fast to the bight of the trawl warp, and putting this on the capstan heave in on it. Of course they must in the meantime get their vessel well off the wind so that the warp leads aft otherwise it might run under the keel without helping to wear the ship.

b. To stay the trawl around

For various reasons it is often desirable to *stay the vessel around* instead of wearing with it. This operation is thus described by Olsen—

"First put the helm hard up and turn the vessel off before the wind, then pass the warp round the bow to shift the rigging onto the dummy. Then stopper the bight on the lee bow let go to windward put the helm a-lee, and when the foresail is a-back drop the mizzen peak let go the bight of the warp on the starboard bow, and when the vessel has paid off before the wind, and brought the warp aft I would bring her slowly to."

c. To drop a vessel around with her trawl out

He would drop the vessel round as follows — I would bring the vessel slowly to the wind with the foresail down, and when on the wind lash the helm a-lee. As soon as the vessel is steady I pass the bight of the warp round the bow in the same way as in staying, or I would pass a good guy round and heave the trawl warp upon the starboard bow, then I take the bight of the warp aft on the dummy and secure it slack away my guy and set a piece of the foresail aback. In this way the vessel will gradually bring the gear off the weather side steady her and secure all.

N. B.—This system is only used in bad weather when it is needful to bring the ship on the other tack."

(h) To catch the Vessel around with a Weather Tide.

To perform this evolution he says: "I should let the vessel sag to windward of the gear by lashing the helm half a'lee. When well off, she will then bring the trawl warp across the stern, which ultimately cause the vessel to come round on the other tack. I then trim the sails immediately and lash the helm a-lee. This can be done in fine weather."

(i) TO PREVENT A VESSEL FROM CATCHING AROUND

when towing with weather tide and light wind, and the gear to windward of her gear, Olsen says: "I should bring the warp aft on her quarter, pass it round the stern and make it fast to the trawl, heave taut with the capstan, slack the trawl warp, and tow with it under the lee."

(j) THE WORKING OF THE TRAWL.

The methods of shooting a beam trawl and of managing it while having been discussed, it seems desirable and proper that something should be said of the action or working of a trawl on the bottom [illegible] a description is given of how it is hove up, etc.

From what has been said of the trawl it will be obvious that this implement is designed more especially for the capture of such fish as live on the bottom, and which are generally denominated "ground fish." Among these various species of flat fish—several of which are the highly prized of the European sea fishes—are perhaps more easily and surely caught by a beam trawl than in any other way.

With rare exceptions all the soles, turbot, and plaice brought to market are caught by the trawl. The various kinds of skate are also obtained by the same means, [illegible] and rays. The [illegible] habits of all these fish, there is very little chance of their escape when once the trawl beam has passed over their heads.

The movement of the trawl through the water when it is being towed keeps the net distended and the back raised some distance from the ground; and as it is traveling with the tide, and the natural tendency of fish is to head the current, it follows that they are liable to be overtaken, when their first impulse would doubtless be to attempt to escape by darting in the direction they were heading; this action on their part would take them directly into the cod end.

"Should the fish, however, by any chance turn around and go towards the mouth of the net, there would probably be a considerable distance to go before they would be clear, as the ground rope sweeps the bottom from the [illegible] of the two head irons to a distance of 50 feet backwards to the bosom of the net, and thus whole space [illegible]

[illegible] Sea [illegible]
Deep-Sea Fishing and Fishing Boats, [illegible]

closed above by the boom, and at the sides of the wing, is no possible escape except... how can you get a fish under the foot rope... as it moves over... so far, and is it that most of... made... a... not as... again try to hide themselves almost... as... they do not bury themselves... deeply, they still... on the ground rope, if... In... as... so... close to the bottom... as... but... the same for which... with... trally rise and pass the net above it... country, they dart to avoid the mouth in... in... that direction, but they rise... will probably... some before they can get clear... an opportunity to take effectual... net... as they pass inside.

It is generally pretty well ascertained that... is... trawl much faster for the experiment, fish than... In the fishes on that... exposed... and... soles the haddock and... generally low then... depths...

Mr. Sims says... it is important... ground for soles on the ground rope... to drag... as a rule... but if we are fishing for hake or haddock... for sheet... it is better... that scrapes the ground.

Of course, this increase of the line... when the trawl... ground renders the escape of those fish much less... would otherwise be... since the net is kept almost clear of... barely skimming... which seems to be necessary on other bottom... species... But although the trawl... the bottom, it requires only a... breeze of wind and very... speed on... vessel to obtain... speed. On the British smacks, according to Holdsworth... of lower studding sails is frequently... open... a weather side... and so forth under... sails. The... all but it to stand under a... apparatus... a large vessel lying over to the breeze... appears... water when nearly with all the help of a... and a favorable tide, she is not going faster over the ground.

From the foregoing... it... an... we implement for the capture of ground fish... comparatively shallow water where this bottom... operated... worked with the best success, is... as... it has previously been said concerning its... in... grounds where it is closed operated...

7. HEAVING OF THE TRAWL

Under ordinary circumstances the trawl is hove up when the tide has done running, if it is day time, or when the limit of a fishing ground is reached and it is not practicable to tow back over it on the other tack. As a rule, the North Sea fishermen tow all night if the conditions are favorable—tacking or wearing the trawl round with the change of tide—haul in the morning, dress box, and deliver the fish on board of the carrier, and then, if the day is short, work to windward for another night's drift over the ground. In summer the trawl is usually shot during the early part of the day, as well as at night, and hove up in the afternoon, thus two hauls are made instead of one. If fleeting, as is the general way in summer, the admiral signals when to shoot and when to heave up the gear. However, it frequently happens that a smack's trawl may catch afoul on the bottom, and therefore it is necessary to heave it up whether it has been out long or not, and it is often found desirable to get the gear at midnight and make a second "shot," especially when fleeting.

The following description of the method adopted on board of the *Willie and Ada* will give a fair idea of how the trawl is hove up and got on board of the ordinary North Sea sailing trawler in moderate weather.

About 5 o'clock p. m. the fourth hand, a lad of some seventeen years of age, who was on deck, shouted down the companion that he thought the admiral was heaving. The captain instantly ran on deck, but headed, and satisfying himself that the report made by the watch was correct, came back into the cabin and called all hands; the men, in obedience to his call, soon making their appearance on deck. When they were all up the jib-sheet was cased off, the helm put down, and two or three of the men shoved forward on the trawl-warp until it was placed on the roller. Two turns of the hawser had previously been put on the capstan, and as the vessel swung slowly head to the wind—helped by the mizzen which the skipper hauled to windward—the cranks were shipped on the capstan preparatory to heaving; while the cook jumped down into the hold to receive and coil the warp as it came in. When the vessel tacked—which she was assisted in doing by the trawl-warp being so far forward—she "went back over her gear," as it is called, slacking up the hawser, which the men hove in as rapidly as possible until it was tightened again, when the foresail was hauled down, the helm was put a lee, and the smack brought on the other tack. In this way the skipper continued tacking the vessel, making short boards back and forth, working up to the gear; while the men at the capstan hove away briskly until all the slack was in. The object of this maneuver was to get in the greater part of the warp with as little labor as possible, since of course it is far easier to heave in slack haw-

---

If the vessel is fishing alone, or single-boating, as it is called, the fish are dressed and packed in bins or pens in the hold.

HEAVING UP THE TRAWL.

see that it would be if there was a strain upon it. Therefore, as the vessel stood back and forth the men at the capstan reported, in answer to the captain's inquiries, if the warp was "coming" after her, and if so, another tack was made. When the slack of the warp was in, the vessel was hove to on the port tack, with the jib sheet eased off and the helm lashed down, and the captain proceeded to assist in heaving. As the capstan turned the bridles were inside the trawl-warp roller.* The end of the dandy bridle was then cast off from the trawl warp by the captain, who took it aft, passed it through the chock on the port side of the taffrail, and thence to the dandy winch, upon which it was fixed so that it would wind in without slipping.

The captain generally heaves in most of the dandy bridle alone; sometimes he is assisted by one of the crew, and for the last few feet two or three men may lend him a hand. In the meantime, as soon as the end of the trawl warp comes inside of the capstan, the after bridle is unshackled, its end taken off the capstan, and thrown on deck, or two or three loose turns taken with it around the dummy. This bridle has a piece of spun yarn wound around near its end, which is a mark whereby it can be told from any other rope at night as well as by day.

While two of the men were unshackling and clearing the after bridle, one hand cast off the fall of the fish tackle, took it to the forward winch, and hove it taut, so that it might be ready for use when needed.

When this was done and the gear was all clear, the men returned to the capstan and hove away on the fore bridle—the skipper at the same time winding in the dandy bridle—until the beam was alongside and a strap, which was spliced into the fore bridle a few feet from the trawl head, was inside the roller. The after end of the beam was then hove snug up to the taffrail and secured. While this was being done two men had hooked the fish tackle into the strap on the fore bridle and began to heave away on the forward winch, lifting the end of the beam and the trawl head over the rail. As it swung in, the trawl head was lowered on deck and secured in its place. If there is any sea going a guy (one end of a rope which is fast to the main shrouds) is rove through the trawl head by one of the men, who takes a turn with the stopper around the main rigging to prevent the forward end of the beam from swinging across deck. The next thing is to get in the net. If there is much weight of fish in the trawl the end of the cod line* is taken to the capstan and the cod end is brought nearly alongside. This is done in order to take the strain off the upper part of the net, which therefore can be more easily gathered in by the men. But when the catch is not large and the sea is smooth, this part of the work is generally omitted. All hands then gather the net in by hand, standing a few

* When there is a strong [illegible] in the manner above described [illegible] the smack [illegible] port tack [illegible] pens that [illegible]

feet apart and lashing over the beam. (See Plate XVII.) As the vessel rolls to windward, a pull is made to get in the slack of the net, which is hauled over the beam and held from slipping back by the men leaning their breasts against it, while they reach out for a new hold. Heavy, hard work this is for five persons to do—two of whom are usually boys—and it frequently happens that the eager looks which are cast over the side to ascertain what success has been met with are unrewarded by the appearance of enough fish in the pockets to indicate a good haul; and it is a bad sign when nothing is said and the bag is got on board without a word.

On the occasion concerning which I am writing, though the catch was small, owing to the trawl having been torn on rough ground, the cod end was not empty by any means. When, therefore, the net had been pulled in so that the cod end was alongside, a selvagee strap was put around the trawl, the fish tackle hooked onto it, and the bag of fish was hoisted up until it would swing in over the rail.

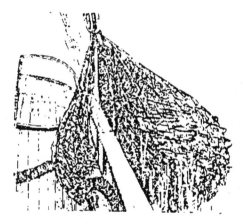

Fig.— Hoisting the cod end.

While it was being raised, a fog rope was taken from the main rigging to the trawl head and made fast to prevent the fish from swinging across deck. When the net was in the poke line, it was cast off, the bottom of the trawl opened, and its contents fell on deck, a sting, writhing, flapping mass. (See Fig. 21.) Nowhere else can one witness such a remarkable scene.

The contents of the net differ according to season and locality, but generally they are of a most varied character—a wonderful exhibition of marine life. Sliding back and forth on the slippery deck, as the vessel rolls in the seaway, are soles, turbot, brill, and plaice, giving vigorous but rather spasmodic slaps on the plank with their tails; here may be seen the writhing body of a conger eel, there the fierce wolf fish, with

Bull. U. S. F. C. 1887.—(To face page 344.)

PLATE XVII.

PULLING IN THE NET.

its jaws armed with wicked-looking teeth, snapping at whatever comes in its way, while prominent in the crowd is one of those wide-mouthed fishing frogs, which some one has called an "animated carpet-bag." These, together with gurnards, iridescent with beautiful color, the vicious dog-fish—always the fisherman's enemy—wriggling about, shells, sea-anemones, sea-corn, etc., constituted a variety of animal life such as is rarely brought together by any other means.

FIG. 24. THE TRAWL'S CONTENTS.

When the net is filled with fish to such an extent that it can not be handled, in the manner above described, a hole is cut in the back, as previously stated, and enough of the catch is bailed out with a dip net to allow of the trawl being taken in. Occasionally it happens that large stones are caught in the trawl and, getting into the "cod," hang down with such great weight that it is difficult, if not impossible, to raise the net in the ordinary way. At such times a long rope slip-strap, or a "clench," made with a running bowline, is put loosely around the trawl and sunk with the deep-sea lead, which is tied to the bight of the strap. When it is low enough it is hauled taut, taken to the capstan and hove up alongside.

The heaving up of a trawl on the single-masted cutters is about the same as that which has been described, the principal difference being that the warp is taken forward and comes in over the bow, the vessel lying head to the wind, the light sails and stay foresail being taken in before the work begins.

Mr. R. L. Ashcroft, of Southport (near Liverpool), England, writing under date of November 14, 1884, gives the following description of the methods of handling a beam trawl on the west coast of England:

"I was out trawling from Fleetwood a fortnight since, with one of the large boats. I should like you to see how easily their gear is worked in comparison with the east-coast boats. Our smacks here fish a 56-foot beam of greenheart, and the boat is only 56-foot keel measurement. But we turn out when we haul the net and haul by the bow, and when we have got the bridle on the winch we take the 'shandy' or spun bridle or, as they call it here, the head rope, which is now made of steel wire rope, to a wink or Spanish windlass aft between the cabin companion and the bulwarks, and get the after end of the net up. Afterwards we winch the forward bridle up and let the after rope bridle surge until we have the forward trawl head almost up, and then hook the fish tackle into a becket on the forward bridle, and take the fall to the winch barrel and coil it on until the iron of the trawl is clear of the rail. Then one of the crew gets hold of the winch barrel under his arm, and, the pawls being lifted up, he watches the roll of the boat and lets the iron come inboard by letting the winch at liberty.

'In the boat I was in there are only four men in the crew, and they made all the nets required.'

The time requisite for heaving up a trawl varies a great deal, depending chiefly on the state of the weather, roughness of the sea, depth of water, direction and strength of the tide, as well as upon whether the capstan is worked by hand or by steam. Captains who have used steam say that under favorable conditions they have got a trawl up—heaving in 120 fathoms of warp—in the short space of fifteen to twenty minutes, while some claim that from twenty to twenty-five minutes is sufficient to heave in the whole warp, even in rough weather.

Heaving a trawl up by hand is not only hard work, but the process is tedious to a degree, rarely occupying less than forty-five to fifty minutes, and sometimes, when the weather is rough and the vessel knocking about, taking between two and three hours.

It will be obvious that when steam trawlers are employed the conditions are quite different from those which obtain on board of a sailing vessel, since a steamer can go in any direction which it may be necessary for her to proceed, and consequently many of the various evolutions which have been described would not be performed. The shooting and hauling of the trawl is done in much the same way, except perhaps that some if not all steamers use a derrick for hoisting one end of the trawl and a davit for the other, and that there may be some difference in the minor details of the method of working. It will be readily understood that, owing to the fact that a steamer is always able to tow in any desired direction, so as to take the utmost advantage of tide and the lay of the ground, as well as to go at the requisite speed at all times, as well as at any other time, vessels of this class are much more effective for working a beam trawl than those which depend solely on sails.

The following account of a trial trip of the new steamer *Caller Ou*, of Granton, Scotland, clipped from the *Scotsman* of December 18, 1883, may be of interest in this connection. One of these exceptional days in December when there is a clear sky overhead, a sharp breeze off the land just sufficient to give a fair lead to a vessel under canvas, and when there has just been restored comparative calm to a sea which had been angry during the storms of a whole week before the *Galley Oor* sailed down the Firth from Granton, with a considerable number of gentlemen on board interested in trawling and deep-sea fishing. It was not until the vessel was off Cinglebeth 18 or 19 miles down the Firth that the trawl was put out. The depth of water was from 11 to 14 fathoms. Of course, the experiments were conducted more with a desire to test the working of the trawl and its appointments than to secure a large haul of fish, and therefore the trawl was kept out during an hour only. When at work under ordinary circumstances these steamers trawl during on an average four hours. Ponderous as the trawl is—the heavy beam, the great net, and the massive iron hoop-like structures which at each end of the beam keep the mouth of the bag or net open—as it sweeps along the bottom of the sea—the working of it by the machinery available was a matter of comparative simplicity and ease. Once cast into the sea, the trawl is dragged along at a speed of between 2 and 3 miles an hour, being attached to the ship by a great wire rope which on Saturday was run out to a length of 75 fathoms. The most interesting part of the trial was when, after the lapse of an hour, the trawl was drawn on board. Here again the steam machinery appeared to work satisfactorily, and in the course of a few minutes the beam and the iron structures were lifted over the side of the ship. The net or bag was still in the sea, and as the crew hauled it on deck its contents were watched with much interest. Soon it was thrown on the deck, containing a couple of hundred weights of white fish—whiting chiefly, with three or four cod and codlings, a couple of skate, a few haddocks, some six or a few flounders, a young turbot and two crabs. This catch, it is obvious, was not a large one for a great trawl such as that described. But the brief period during which it was at work, and the fact that the ground covered was not considered good or the ordinary fishing ground, were said to account for the catch being so small. The fish however were taken up in splendid condition—full of life, and in as clean and a state as might be desired. Whether the short period during which the trawl was at work accounted for it, or whether it was that the condition of the sea bottom was exceptionally favorable, the trawl was laid on the deck wonderfully clean—clear of mud or of any perceptibly objectionable matter—and it was stated that this is the condition in which the trawls are usually taken on board in ordinary weather in the Firth of Forth. Attention was also directed to the quality—the intermixture of immature with mature fish. There were, it was admitted, very few immature fish. There was one codling only 10 inches long, but the other specimens were excellent. There were probably half a dozen very small whitings, one small skate, and one small but not apparently immature flounder. On the whole, however, the apparently

would lead to crowding of vessels at times when it would be dangerous thus to act.

Of course where the fishing grounds are near the home port, fish can easily be sold on market at a port close to the ground. At Brixham, for instance, the single-boating system prevails; moreover this is pursued each skipper of a single vessel choosing his ground, shooting and working his nets, and taking care of the fish and getting it to market. When vessels go to the North Sea the best fishing grounds being a long distance off, speaking from a market point of view as well. It has turned out several days at sea before reaching port. Thus it became difficult before the vessel's fleet worked together in the system which most of them now pursue and thus following the latter being necessitated in order to fish successfully in winter. The trawling vessels from certain ports of the year pursue the system of single-boating in summer and also send vessels from all other ports to the fleet.

A portion of the fleets are accompanied by steam vessels for the ferrying of moving vessels, or steam cutters to carry the trawlers along the east coast of England and elsewhere in the summer. Under this system arrangements being made that a set of vessels to fill their cargoes, and for this purpose a fleet of which are governed by an admiral whose is an experienced and who is known to be an expert fisherman and whose decides where fishing shall be carried on at a given time and locality, and the movements of the other boats are made by signals which the admiral makes. All the vessels must thus shoot and haul their nets at the same time and so together on same tack in obedience to the signals made so that a vessel may be mentioned that by reason of some extent of a vessel.

Flags are used for signaling by day, and rockets or other lights. Each fleet has its own particular code of signal. Vessels which is the following:

<table>
<tr><td>For fishing</td><td></td></tr>
<tr><td>For meeting</td><td></td></tr>
<tr><td>North bound</td><td></td></tr>
<tr><td>Sailing together for fish</td><td></td></tr>
<tr><td>Come away etc.</td><td></td></tr>
</table>

Reports received from the fleet to the
Sea-fisheries for

Mr. Samuel Plimsoll also in his pamphlet on the fisheries of the published in the fact of the fishermen and who are in proportion to these are involved in the are taken on by the fisheries.

Littoral signals by night

For sailing	White rocket at intervals
For trawling	Flare on quarter and a white rocket
For trawling on port tack	Three flares and a red rocket
For trawling on starboard tack	Three flares and a green rocket
For hauling, getting the trawl	Two flares and two white rockets at one time
For laying to	One flare at mast head and one on the quarter with a white rocket

In strong winds the fleet sometimes get scattered, and to facilitate their gathering again without loss of time different places of rendezvous are arranged according to the season of the year, thus:

From February 1 to March 1	Eels end of the Dogger
From March 1 to August 1	On the Horn Reef Light boat
From August 1 to October 1	Clay Deeps
From October 1 to February 1	The Silver Pits

These are well known places to all fishermen

Messrs. Hewett & Co. of London are reputed to have been the first to establish the fleeting system, which they did by arranging to have the large number of smacks they owned combined into one or more fleets that is now were controlled by an admiral, while each day's catch was shipped on board of a swift sailing cutter, which took the fish to market, several of these cutters being in attendance on a fleet so that no time was lost. In all weathers these cutters could be seen hovering about the North Sea fleets, and nowhere in the history of sea fishing life can there probably be found any better examples of courage and hardihood than were exhibited by the crews of these cutters. Winter or summer, so long as they could show any canvas they were driven through all weathers almost to the verge of destruction. The object was to bring the fish to market fresh, and so long as this was accomplished little was thought of hardships, perils, and discomforts, which it is difficult for one to imagine who has not had the experience of continually forcing a passage at sea in a small and deeply laden vessel.

Even at the present time, at least as late as 1880, essentially the same system was carried on from Hull and Grimsby. A limited number — anywhere from ten to thirty — vessels would combine interests and form a fleet, which frequently would be all the property of one firm. These vessels would as a rule all share alike, and the smacks took turns in carrying the catch to port, the admiral's flag being transferred to some other craft when his turn came to go to market. A fleet of this kind is called a cutter fleet, in distinction from the steamer fleets, which

Sometimes the crew of the cutter which received and carries the fish to market pick the cargoes Some put the ice among the fish as on the single boaters, rather than to use boxes. A fleet the cutters which sends its catch to market by one of its own sailing vessels is often called a "boxing fleet," because of the system of packing or fish on land.

are much larger—numbering from seventy-five to one hundred vessels or more—and are attended by several ketch-rigged screw steamers, called steam cutters, which carry out a supply of empty boxes for the fleet, to take the place of those filled with fish, also provisions and letters for the fishermen. But their chief work is to carry the fish from the fleet to the port where they are to be landed, generally London, Grimsby, or Hull.

"One of these cutters is generally leaving every day if the fleet, and the fish which has been caught by the smacks, and has on board of them been packed in boxes, is transferred or handed on the smacks boats to the steam cutter, with which she then goes back to her port of discharge.

Single boats also are in the habit of transferring their fish to these cutters if they chance to fall in with them, and if the cutter has room which is usually the case, the steam cutters charging so much per box for carriage.

"The smacks engaged in the fleeting remain at sea for periods varying from six to eight to ten weeks, when they return to their port there to refit. From Yarmouth there are about six hundred and seventy smacks engaged in 'fleeting,' and from two hundred to two hundred and fifty in single boating in the winter, and in the summer nearly all are engaged in fleeting, and from Grimsby there are about three hundred engaged in fleeting, and one hundred in single boating in summer but none of them go fleeting in winter.

The same necessity exists now for getting the fish to market as soon as possible which led to the hand driving of the sailing carriers, and probably no vessels in the world are forced harder in all weathers than the steam carriers which now attend upon the North Sea fleets, and which rarely fail to make their passages from the most distant fishing grounds to Hull, Grimsby, or London in from thirty-six to forty-eight hours.

A writer in Land and Water who made a cruise in a North Sea trawler in December, and returned to port on a steam carrier, gives the following account of the passage, which will convey a good idea of the conditions under which these vessels frequently make their trips to or from the fishing grounds: "It is impossible to convey even a general idea of the journey back without entering into an amount of nautical detail, for which I have not time. The present age is certainly remarkable for earnestness and zeal in most official men, but there was in the dear, good, clever, brave, old man who brought that vessel home an intensity of devotion which it was positively refreshing to observe. He carried sail when the sea washed all over the ship, and every now and then came down in deluges into the stoke hole, all but extinguishing the furnaces. As to the little cabin, in which we were supposed to live, it was literally drowned, hardly a dry thing being left in it, and the little stove being almost instantly extinguished every time it was lighted

Report to the Board of Trade on the system of deep-sea trawl fishing, etc.

At one time I thought to go in for the luxury of dry boots, so I put a pair before the fire, but in a few moments after a sea struck us, and when I looked down the companion again I saw one boot jammed up right at the foot of the ladder full of water, and the other gaily careering all over the floor upon the bosom of a festive wave, which had floated up all the small gear and so-called furniture, and was then engaged splashing the table underneath. All this time the good skipper never wearied for a moment, and never left the deck except for a few seconds to snatch a mouthful of food, or a drink of cold, creamless tea, which was his only beverage, but forced the vessel through the heavy sea with steam and sail combined until he carried away the gaff, and then with steam alone, until he brought us safely, in what even he owned to being coarse weather, through some of the most dangerous and intricate channels on the coast, and finally reaped the reward of all this great labor and anxiety when he heard from his employers that his cargo was in time for market, and that they were pleased with his exertions.

In regard to the system of fishing pursued by the Grimsby trawlers, Mr. Mudd writes as follows under date of April 29, 1883: "Our vessels fish in fleets principally in summer, and one or two fleets continue all winter. A fleet of about one hundred and fifty smacks are attended upon by four or five steam carriers of 170 to 150 tons register, fifty to sixty horse-power engines, which carry their fish to market in ice, so that the smacks carry no ice, they [the smacks] go on the grounds for eight or ten weeks fishing, then come home for a week and off again. This is the most profitable system of fishing.

"Steam trawling is great at Grimsby just now. I helped to form a company last year. We have two boats which have been at work three months with fair success. We are going in for four more."

Steam trawlers as a rule go on the single-boating system generally carrying on their operations within 20 to 60 miles from the land, from which distance they can easily reach the markets while their catch is in good condition. Sometimes they act in the capacity of carriers and trawlers too, fishing in a fleet the product of which as well as their own catch they take to market. It may be explained in this connection that it sometimes happens that sailing trawlers can do little fishing for several days at a time because of a continuance of calm weather. On such occasions the steam trawler finds her opportunity, and by the time that the fleet gets a good day's fishing she may have obtained a large catch herself, which adds materially to the income she may derive from the carriage of fish.

When single boating, writes Dunell, "they often average £60 per week in their gross catch. During the summer they act as carriers to a large fleet of sailing smacks. After being out about a week they will catch £40 to £60 worth of fish themselves, and at the same time bring in a cargo in boxes from the sailing smacks. This arrangement is found lucrative to the company and gives advantage to sailing vessels, as it insures the fish being delivered in good condition and obviates the necessity of the smacks making long passages to from their port, often with contrary winds. The advantage of system to that of having steam carriers proper is, however, in weather, frequent in such seasons, the smacks cannot work to it so that the carriers have no fish to take round, and thus lie unemployed, and the other incurring loss. On the other hand steam trawler is enabled to work without aid, and may land which will be, perhaps, additionally valuable on account of the forced idleness of the other vessels.

Higher prices are generally obtained for fish which reach market by the steam carriers than for those brought in by the boats, though this is not invariable rule.

It may occasionally happen, according to the report on the Trade, that smacks fleeting are obliged to keep one fish on board several days on account of the rough weather preventing their conveyed to the steam cutter, and as the fleeting vessels do not carry like the single boats it is quite possible under such circumstances that the fish may arrive in inferior condition. One witness stated he had known smacks men to fill the steam cutters boxes with fish a single fleeting smack in order to enhance the price.

The fleeting system is preferred by the owners, though carriers are in favor of single boating. It is claimed that the fleeting system more profitable, that it is necessary for the owners and the fish should be not only quick and large, but subject to as little loss as possible. Whilst, however, a difference of 20 per cent in the may make a difference to the owner of a fair profit or a decided only makes to the men sailing on shares a reduction of six from £1 12s per week, and to the men on wages it makes no difference at all. Therefore, it is not perhaps to be wondered at that the men prefer the system of single boating, and there several reasons urged by them against fleeting. Chief among these objections hard and perilous work of transferring the fish and the much time that they are obliged to be absent from home.

The Duke of Edinburgh in his excellent paper on the Sea Fisheries gives a graphic picture of the dangers incident to transferring as carried on under the fleeting system, which he concludes by saying

"No one will deny the great importance to the owners of smacks getting their fish to market in a saleable condition, but they ought to effect this object without exposing the fishermen to dangers as I have above indicated, but against such means of preventing have as yet been devised or adopted. I have alluded to the subject here as an illustration of the necessity of a fishermen's act, and leave it without expressing my opinion in favor of or against such inquiry being made on the occasion on which a fisheries vessel turns to port having lost any of her crew whilst at sea. This inquiry, it seems to me, should be conducted by a competent authority whose duty it would be to satisfy himself and place on record the manner in which the life was lost, whether by one of these preventable causes or not. For, at present the fact of a life being lost at sea is the only record which exists, no matter how it occurred.

"To sum up the advantages or otherwise of these two systems, says the report of the Hull investigation, we are of opinion that the 'single boating' system, whilst insuring to the men less hardship and possibly conducing to instruct them in a more perfect knowledge of their business as fishermen is also productive of a great waste of fish. The fleeting system, on the contrary, is calculated to secure a more regular and continuous supply in a fresher state. We are not inclined to attach much importance to the argument that in 'single boating' there is less danger from the congregating together of a number of vessels. We have it in evidence that a great number of 'single boating' vessels are found together, and we are of opinion that the fact of their then sailing each at his own will without the regularity insured by acting in concert, as in a fleet is of itself an increased danger. A single boat getting mixed up with a fleet would have a similar effect. The danger of collision to these vessels has been shown by numerous witnesses to occur chiefly in fine weather and in the daytime, not owing to circumstances connected with fleeting per se, but to a habit amongst the skippers of visiting one another in such weather when trawling can not be carried on for want of wind, and leaving their smacks in charge of the boys. The same results may ensue when two or more single boats meet together under similar circumstances."

CARE OF FISH—DRESSING FISH, ETC.

The various kinds of fish taken in trawls are classified under two general heads of "prime" and "offal," while all other material, such as invertebrates, radiates, etc., receives the name of "scrup" or "scrush." "Prime" fish are the choicest varieties, which bring the highest price in market, such for instance is the sole, turbot, brill, and dory; while cheaper and less desirable species, such as haddock, gurnards, plaice, flounders, skate, etc., are called "offal."

"Red mullet must be excepted, however, says Holdsworth, "for, although not strictly coming under the head of 'prime,' they are what the Billingsgate salesmen look upon as 'West End' fish."

The fish are dressed, sorted, and packed away as soon as is practicable after the trawl is taken up. As has been stated, the fish fall on deck from the cod end in a slimy, struggling mass, and, if there be any sea, they go scurrying and sliding from side to side as the vessel rolls back and forth. The fishermen use ordinary clasp knives, or what are usually termed "jack knives," of a large size, for dressing the catch, each

PLATE XVIII.

DRESSING THE FISH.

man being provided with a [illegible] these may be carried in his [illegible] when not using it, and which he employs for various other pur[poses] for which a knife may be required, such as filling his pipe, cutting, etc. Dressing fish, so far as we have had an opportunity of observing it, is carried on in a [illegible] way differing very much from the [illegible] of the methods employed by American fishermen. The men [illegible] in a stooping position, picking the fish up from the deck [illegible] down and grab whatever comes first to their hands as the fish [are] [illegible] back and forth when the vessel rolls. The fish are simply [e]viscerated, such as are dressed, for it often happens that [illegible] certain species are not even gutted. If it be a round fish, the cod, haddock, etc., a slit is made in the belly, the viscera pulle[d] and the [illegible] cut off where it joins the gills. If a flat fish, [a] cut across on the upper or eye side of the abdominal cavity, [the] intestines are pulled out with the right hand, the operator [holding] the fish by its head in his left hand. The fish are packed [illegible] with the white or belly side up, and the slit does not show, [and] blood or water that may be in it will escape. As the fish are [illegible] they are sometimes, though not always, roughly sorted into [illegible] of prime and offal, but more attention is paid to the culling [illegible] whole have been washed. Up to this point there is little diffe[rence] in the methods employed on board of either the single boaters o[r] [ves]sels that are fleeting, except it may be on [illegible] like those [of] Brixham, the catch of which is rarely dressed at all, but taken [illegible] landed in small baskets.

If the vessel is single boating, the fish are as previously mentio[ned] stowed in bulk in pens or "pounds" made in the hold by shutt[ers,] adjustable bulkheads. The prime fish are generally kept separa[te].

If, however, the vessel is fleeting, the fish are disposed of in a [dif]ferent manner. As soon as they are dressed and washed [illegible] empty boxes or "trunks" are taken on deck, each smack always [has a] supply of these, and the fish are carefully packed in them according [to] grade, after which a string is tied across the top opening to pr[event] the contents from falling out while being transshipped. Each box [is la]beled with a wooden tag on which is the name of the vessel [and] of the salesman on shore to whom it is consigned, while a note or [dupli]cate bill of lading, showing the number of boxes of each kind [illegible] going from the smack, is made out to send with the shipment. [The] fish are now ready to be taken on board of the carrier, for [illegible] whole fleet of smacks has gathered in the morning, numbering [illegible] [illegible] fleet may be from seventy to [illegible] hundred [illegible] vessels. The operation of "boarding" or ferrying the fish fro[m] catcher to a steam carrier has been so graphically described by [a cor]respondent of "Land and Water" that I can do no better than to [quote] it here:

The boat is then launched over the side, no matter how heav[y] so it may be—and the necessary number of men, generally three, jump in and their mates on board hand them down the boxes, which when full weigh about one hundred weight each. Sometimes there are very few boxes to go off, in certain cases none at all, at other times there may be as many as fifteen or twenty, or, in the event of the smack having been unable to send any for a day or two previously, there may occasionally be more, but this is not very usual. The boat is then towed behind the smack with a painter of about 10 fathoms in length, and the smack makes sail either ahead or astern of the steamer, or sometimes round and round until she has got it into such a position that they are likely to be able to reach by themselves when she lets go and they make their own way with oars. The whole of this proceeding is little short of wonderful; in fact it is impossible for any one to understand what these men can do with their boats without seeing it. A common, awkward-looking row-boat is first pushed over the gunwale into a heavy sea, and almost before the fact of its having got safely in without being swamped is realized a man has somehow swarmed over the side and got on board, a turn of the painter is taken round a belaying pin on deck, two other men follow the first, and the crew hand in the fish, the sea all the time rising and falling to a height of 18 feet or 19 feet, and not one of those engaged appearing to take the slightest notice of it or in any way betraying the smallest consciousness that there is a sea at all. Then the towing with a long rope, which I have never seen before, is most remarkable, and the effect of a number of vessels running down together towards the cutter, each every now and again on the crest of one wave while its boat is on the crest of the next and the long painter is taut in the mud in between, is something quite beyond one's ordinary experience and forms a rather interesting study. The quietness too with which they break about among each other in the heavy seas is somewhat instructive, no special lookout or symptom of anxiety being anywhere apparent, and yet all giving each other clear berths and no collisions happening. Verily, great is the confidence inspired by real knowledge and constant practice. And now the boats approach the carrying vessel, the men in them sing out "Let go!" those on board reply "All gone!" and then the towing begins and up and down they go on seas so heavy that every now and then they are lost to sight for an uncomfortable length of time. At last they approach the vessel, and though, to a man accustomed even to yacht, he ship

This very severe work is the trade of a fortnight season carried on in almost all states of weather and seas, the peril attached to the work as I assure you for a berth in the midst of a season. Any risk of the possibility of danger to themselves, they had of a trawler's boat work, its crews and crew to fix up a boat I had long to sit on the deck of weather and the main.

In the scatterer and struggles of a large number of these trawl cutters, each of which is striving for the best place or in the subsequent endeavors of each to their own vessels, accidents are necessarily of frequent occurrence, too often attended by loss of life.

BOXING THE FISH.

posed that they must be swamped in coming alongside, they come on
all the same, not even keeping a lookout, so far as one can observe, but
running in every direction full tilt onto the ship, and as each boat
touches, a man watches his chance, and just when the boat rises takes
hold of the rail and swarms
up over it and fairly tumbles
on the deck, holding one end
of the long painter in some
way, either in his hands, under
an arm, or sometimes in his
teeth.

FIG. 22. BOARDING FISH.

"He picks himself up at once, rushes on to the shrouds or to a belay-
ing-pin, takes a turn, and sings out, 'All fast!' and then one of his
mates in the boat, who has been paying out, hauls short on the painter
until he gets abreast of the waist of the ship or some other part that
may be vacant; the men in the boat immediately hand up the boxes
one by one, their own man receives them over the rail and tosses them
on deck, then puts his delivery note into a basket in the galley, and his
work is done. It is the business of each smack to deliver her own cargo
on the deck, and no help is given for the purpose, not even in the small
matter of making fast a painter or helping in a trunk, and the short
time occupied in the operation, as well as the apparent certainty and
safety of the whole proceeding, are, to say the least, surprising. Indeed
it seems little short of miraculous that in a sea with a rise and fall of
quite 10 feet some eighty or ninety open boats should be launched overboard, manned and loaded, towed and rowed a considerable distance,
brought alongside a vessel, unloaded, brought back, and hoisted on
board again without a single accident, yet I saw this done without anything approaching to a misadventure, and from the general bearing of
all concerned I could observe that there was no anxiety whatever on
the subject."

Notwithstanding no accident occurred on the occasion referred to above, and although the fishermen exhibited no anxiety, it is nevertheless a fact that the ferrying of fish is accompanied with a great deal of risk and peril, and it not unfrequently happens that men are drowned while engaged in this service. Concerning this the following report was made to the Board of Trade. During the progress of the investigations held before us it was repeatedly shown that this operation of shooting the fish is conducted without regard to order or system of any kind whatever. So soon as the steam cutter arrives at the fleet, each smack hastens to send its boat alongside first to fetch stores, letters etc., and empty boxes for future use, and again to load the full ones on board the steam cutter. The smacks sail up close to the steam cutter some on one tack and some on the other, dropping their boats alongside as they pass the head of her, where they lay to waiting to pick up their boat again. Many boats by this means get congregated alongside the steam cutter at the same time, and a struggle ensues as to who shall unload his fish first. The result is that boats are frequently smashed and sometimes capsized, occasionally entailing loss of life to the hands in them. Some of the smacks also are in the habit of running so close to these boats that a wash is produced, which increases the danger. In the Hull and Grimsby fleets the men who man the boats discharge the boxes onto the deck of the steamer and then generally lower them into the hold where the steamer's crew stow them away, assisted by a certain number of smack hands who are paid a gratuity for this work. Elsewhere it is the rule for the boxes to be placed only on the deck of the steamer by the boat's crew.

It may be mentioned here that attempts have been made to devise some other means for transferring the fish from the catcher to the carrier. A sketch was exhibited in the British section at the International Fisheries Exhibition at London showing how the transfer could be made by means of an endless rope working between a smack and a cutter, the fish boxes being tied to the rope, and pulled on board the steamer through the water. Laboring under the mistaken idea that the beam trawl fishery is carried on in American waters, Mr. John Bland of London, who it would appear, is the deviser of this scheme, addressed a letter to the President of the United States, in which, after speaking of the danger attending the boarding of fish, he takes occasion to say: I would suggest that at a distance of 60 or 100 yards the collecting steamer throw by rocket a slight line to the smack. By means of this line the smack would drive to itself an endless rope, to be arranged over a loose block 6 or 8 feet above the deck. A box or barrel of fish would be attached to the lower part of the rope by means of a simple hook, then dropped overboard, and drawn to the steamer by steam power. A few minutes immersion would not do the slightest harm to the boxes, and as the water would support the greater part of the weight, a dozen packages of fish might be attached to the rope at the some time with a short distance between them, say one box for every 6 yards of rope. By this means I believe the catch could be transferred, day or night, and in almost all weather, with a tenth part of the present labor, and no risk to life or boats, as quickly as the steamer could haul the boxes up her sides. A supply of empty cases could be sent to the smack in the same manner.

Whether this plan will be found feasible or not, it is difficult to say. We could not learn that any practical test of it has been made. But the difficulty of keeping two vessels at the proper distance to work in a heavy sea without danger of collision would unquestionably be found very great, and then only one could work at a time, which would be of small consequence when a hundred others were waiting to discharge their fish.

In a remarkably brief space of time the steamer's deck is filled with boxes, which as fast as possible are being transferred from the deck to the hold, this transfer being actively conducted by the carrier's crew, who are sometimes assisted by the men from the fishing smacks. Each steamer has a compartment in which enough ice is carried to preserve the fish. This place is called the "ice house" and is connected with the main hold—where the fish are stowed—by a hole in the bulkhead which can be opened and closed as required. While part of the steamer's crew are busied in passing down and stowing the "trunks" of fish, others are hard at work converting the blocks of ice into the particles, and when a tier of boxes have been stowed in the hold a layer of fine ice is thrown on them, and so the work goes on until the hold is filled with fish enough, with alternate layers of fish and ice, a few baskets of the latter being thrown on top of the last tier of boxes. Over all is laid a cloth, and then the hatches are closed and securely battened down.

In the meantime the confusion incident to getting the fish on board and the chaffing of the smackmen who crowd the steamer's deck, has ceased, most if not all of the boats have returned to their respective vessels which may now be seen stretching off together in obedience to the admiral's sailing signal, while the carrier's bow is pointed for port and no time is lost in getting all sail set that she will carry, for no effort is spared to increase the speed.[1]

II.—MARKETING THE CATCH.—FISH CARRIAGE, ETC.

1. *Landing the fish at Billingsgate.*—The arrival of a steam carrier in the Thames is immediately telegraphed to London from the signal stations near the river's mouth, and Billingsgate makes all necessary provision for receiving and disposing of her cargo. As soon as she arrives her load is rapidly transferred from the steamer's hold to the

[1] It does not always happen that every vehicle has a smack's equipment. It often happens for a carrier to go to market with as much as she can carry, until another day's supply be obtained.

DISCHARGING A STEAM CARRIER AT BILLINGSGATE.

small costermonger to postpone his visit to Billingsgate till he has disposed of his purchases of the previous day."

Such are some of the features connected with the selling of fish at Billingsgate. Elsewhere mention is made of the methods of receiving, selling, and shipping of fish at Grimsby, which differ somewhat from those in vogue at London.

Fish sale at Brixham.—In the summer of 1883, while making a brief visit to Brixham, the writer had an opportunity of learning something of the methods of trawling as pursued from that port. Since the description of the care of fish marketing, etc., which we have given applies more particularly to the methods adopted by the North Sea fishermen and at the larger ports, it may be of interest to say something here of how the business is conducted at Brixham. The vessels employed from Brixham are mostly single-masted cutters which fish not far from its harbor, though a number of ketch-rigged trawlers which go to the North Sea are owned there and for about two months in summer a few Brixham boats fish off Tenby in Wales. With the exception of those fishing in the North Sea each of these vessels carry a crew of three men and a boy. The vessels fishing about home stay in harbor on Sunday, as a rule. They generally land their catch every day—usually in the morning—sometimes twice a day when the conditions are favorable. They carry no ice. As soon as the trawl is got on board in the morning the vessel is headed for Brixham and all necessary sail is set. The fish are assorted and packed in small baskets called "pads," of which there are two sizes one holding about 10 or 12 pounds, and the other double that quantity.

If the weather is fine the cutter heaves to outside the pier, the boat is got out, the fish put into her and two of the crew take the "lot" to the harbor where they land their cargo at the market. As soon as the fish are sold—sometimes before—the men return to their vessel that, in the mean time, has been jogging outside, and which immediately heads off for the fishing ground again. If the wind blows fresh this cannot be done, therefore the smack anchors outside if the wind is off the land, otherwise she goes to Dartmouth, Torquay or Plymouth."

The baskets have the vessel's mark attached to them, so that they may be known. All fish are sold at auction to the highest bidder, and not at a Dutch auction as at Grimsby, where the *last* bidder takes

The British Fish Trade, by Sir Spencer Walpole, lieutenant-governor of the Isle of Man, pp. —.

The report, under a head of Sea-fishing on the Southwest Coast, by F. C. Wilson, as it appeared in the London Field of February 28, 1885, the following is stated with regard to trade to the Brixham smacks going to other ports: "The largest number of trawlers delivering fish at Plymouth during the past week was a hundred and two, thirty or forty of the vessels were from Brixham the whole of the smacks being over the North being a little under seventy in number. The increase in number of vessels delivering fish at Plymouth was owing to a strong east wind. At Torquay the largest number of vessels delivering fish was only thirty-two, a small number for this important fishing port.

SELLING FISH AT BILLINGSGATE MARKET.

whatever is being sold. The sales at Fleetwood begin at 9 o'clock a.m. and continue as long as fish arrives to be sold.

They are conducted by a number of salesmen who dispose of the fish as fast as it arrives (?) on the usual basis, the usual commission of sales and dock fee. The greater part of the fish goes south(?) and mostly to country trade, the greater part of the congested landings going to Manchester. A number of women were at work cleaning and packing the poorer grades of fish into casks and haddocks which are hawked about the interior towns, while a somewhat better grade was being packed in carts and wagons with ice; these, as it were sold were for sale at bargains.

4. *Shields as a fish market.*—Shields is of late years come considerable importance as a market for trawled fish, since it now has a large fleet of steam trawlers.

The following account of the arrival and effect of steamers at the Shields fish market, and the sale and shipment of their cargoes is quoted from the London Fish Trades Gazette of October 17, 1889:

When mild September gives place to mild October, and the fish of the herring boats has spread its brown wings and disappeared north or south, as the case may be, then the steam trawler seems to settle itself down to business to practically take sole possession once more of the fishquay at Shields, just like some party who had been bewildered and harassed by summer visitors and was right glad to get rid of them. There is a wealth of all that is picturesque in the herring fleet at anchor and their doings, but the steam trawler on a dull winter's day gives you a picture that is thrilling—one that serves to make you totally oblivious to the keenest blast from the North Sea when you have screwed up the courage to steal from out your warm blankets and venture down to the low lights in the early morning. A beautiful companion picture is to be had in the scene on the quay after the fish is landed and salesmen are busy laying themselves hoarse while big consignments are being hurried away and preservers are in full tongue. Being anxious to look on the scene as a whole from beginning to end, the writer the other morning found a crisp saucily cold northerly to secure shelter from a biting sea breeze made to the lee of a pile of casks and boxes beneath the huge shed which serves as despatching department to the various depots. There was little else that indicated the scene of life and bustle which was soon to follow. Everybody seemed to be bent on shelter like myself, and the spacious boarding on the quay was tenanted only as yet, and ferries were here and there. Eventually there was some commotion as one or two muffled-up men who looked as if something to do would come as a treat toward the extreme end of the jetty which juts out into the river and gives a view down the harbor and out to sea. There they stood, hands thrust elbow deep into their pockets and, sucking vigorously at local twist tobacco gazed out onto the waters. What's the matter with those fellows?

looked on in neglect.   There is only looking if anything's coming
was the reply.   Presently signs of animation amongst the group drew
others along myself amongst the number.   The first trawler was in
the offing.   However, there was some dispute on the point.   I tell
you its not she -- says one.   Its the tug -- says another, and
so on until one raised, look at individual who puts his eyesight against
the younger of the crowd exclaims. It is the -- There's her dead-
rick.   And there's her beam.   The object of dispute seemed some
miles away.   I watched her for some half hour growing larger and
larger, now swaying to all appearances in the water up to the top of
her funnel, descending again bold relief on the top of a wave.   Several
others had been neglected in the meanwhile, and all were noted trawlers.
The first one seemed bent on getting first to the river, and from and
great large rolls of black smoke came from her funnel mingling with
occasional puffs of steam which rose from her valves as she lifted to
the seas these demonstrations of activity bringing forth the remark,
"He's firing up now boys."   At length she came between the piers and
into the smooth water of the river, and with her paddles slowly club-
bing the water drew alongside the quay.   It was low water, and from
the quay above we soon all now could be had of her decks.   Her black
funnel was peppered like a washing cake several feet upwards, where
the spray had struck it, and here the white salt had baked on.   The
fires she had evidently been a good one, for the sorting of it up had
not been completed.   Several of her hands encased in oilskins and
looking like so many lobsters standing erect and were busy putting the
cargo to rights.   Her tow deck was divided into pens like a cattle
market each kind of fish being stuck amongst its own kith and kin.
During the whole of this operation the quick pulsations of the donkey
pump were heard, and one of the hands vigorously plied the hose pipe
right and left as cleaning or polishing up of fish deck boxes and boards.
A pile of baskets were then put aboard, and filled so much into each
as far as the smaller fish would go.   These with the larger fish brought
up in twos and threes were then railed on to the quay and taken
charge of by assistants of the salesman who usually had the "selling"
of the fare.   Whilst this was going on other trawlers had arrived
one after the other, and assembled round the quay, until there was a
general hubbub uproar fish going on, the accompaniment of donkey
pumps working, horses rattling on and and out shouts from the men
ashore or afloat.

The scene on the quay was now one of great animation.   The fish
had been were being from the trawlers and placed in various lots upon
the quay.   The larger fish were sorted up into groups, for instance
you might see two or three cod or two or three ling lying together
and here and there a congered ling hooking cat fish halibut, turbot
or monster skate.   The place soon reeking whitings were remained
in baskets.   It was a sight to see this mustering of the tribes of the

far so far as the success of the British beam-trawl fishery is concerned, but for obvious reasons these questions to states will not be discussed at length in these notes. As has been shown large quantities of fish are taken direct from the fishing fleets in the North Sea to London; the amount of fish thus carried from sea to Billingsgate has been estimated by competent authority at 42,000 tons yearly, while 90,000 tons reach London by land.

Owing to the fact, writes Mr. Plimsoll, that Grimsby and Hull are so much nearer the fishing ground than London is by far the larger portion is carried into these ports and thence off by night trains to London.

The more valuable kinds of fish on being landed are packed into large boxes or hampers, but the kit haddocks are put loose into what are called machines. These machines are long boxes lined with lead, some 15 feet long by 5 feet broad and 2 feet deep, which are divided internally into four equal spaces each of which holds half a ton of fish and the machine is carried on the railway on a truck or wagon with low sides. On arriving in London these machines are lifted bodily from the railway wagon by a powerful hydraulic crane, lowered onto a strong street trolly, and drawn by horses into Thames street where they form a line sometimes a quarter of a mile long, and these are the things (and these only) as any one may see any day by going into Thames street that cause the obstruction and overcrowding. As continuing the less valuable fish they wait until they are continuing the prime, which is sold first are unloaded. The detention is sometimes for eight or nine hours; the average over a long period was found to be four hours and forty-nine minutes, so that the average detention of the tanks containing off-fish is probably not under six hours. Some cod and other kinds of prime are carried in these tanks or machines but the quantity is very small indeed compared with that of the kit haddock—the great bulk of cod etc. being packed in boxes and hampers.

Much fault has been found with the rates charged for the transportation of fish by rail, it being claimed by interested parties that these are excessive. As however this is somewhat of a local matter, it does not seem necessary that anything more than a passing allusion should be made to it.

It is proper however to remark that the carriage of fish notwith-

[footnote text, largely illegible]
Fisheries of the sea ... We are ... that so ... of the fish brought to London are carried ... these ... ports. On the contrary it seems as the central station of the ... in ... of machines ... day is sure ... only to become larger. On the other hand ... to ... and ... is the conclusion attained at ... It is to be ... to ... not be ... and sold later or at more places than two at the railway terminal ... at two places. In exchange is that unless more perfect distribution ... the fish ... ...from ... for England in the ... and London is in a ... a smaller extent Manchester and Liverpool are the markets to which nearly the whole of England is supplied ... the ... and London is much less ... to a great extent the center of supply.
Fish Trades Gazette June 2 188-

standing complaints that have been made concerning delays, have reached a high state of perfection, and it would no doubt to the advantage of the American fish trade if several thousand tons to be employed in the United States, as in Great Britain, for transporting fish. According to the Duke of Edinburgh only about 100 tons were condemned at Billingsgate in the year 1881, as unfit for [...], a large proportion of which was shell-fish. This he thinks strange for the system of carriage, as London receives annually a supply of 115,000 tons of fish.

1. METHOD OF DIVIDING THE PROFITS.

There are certain local differences for the division of the money obtained from sales of fish caught by trawling-smacks, but the following table showing the apportionment of a trawling-smack's earnings of £800, furnished by Mr. Sims of Hull, and published in the report of the inquiry at Hull by the Board of Trade, will give each of the methods adopted for settlement at the large trawling ports of the North Sea.

Assuming that a smack earns £800 to be settled out, that is [...] for division between owners and crew:

The skipper's share is	[...]
The second hand's share is	[...]
Provisions found by owners for the three other hands, say	[...]
Wages for three other hands, say, £1 [...] per week	[...]
Insurance, say, on £800, the assessed value of the vessel at [...]	[...]
Repairs for wear and tear of vessel, sails, spars, fishing-gear, etc., [...] bottom, etc.	[...]
Interest on £800 at 5 per cent.	[...]
Depreciation of vessel	[...]

The skipper's share	[...]
Less provisions	[...]

	115
	[...]

Second hand's share	[...]
Less provisions	[...]

The foregoing statement suggests the approximate earnings of a [...] class North Sea trawler and her crew. As a matter of course considerable variation in the amount earned by different vessels, some stocking more than £800 and others much less. The average earnings of sailing trawlers according to Duncll for the three [...] ending in 1885 was £660 per annum.

The earnings of steam trawlers are much greater as a rule. The steam trawlers belonging to the Grimsby company for the year ending February 1883, averaged £2,500 to each vessel, but as these carry more men and their expenses are necessarily much larger, the crew's share is not so large in proportion as the difference in the relative stocks would seem to indicate.

In conversation with the skipper of a Brixham smack, I was told that 100 pounds of fish exclusive of prisers is considered a good day's catch for one of the trawlers working off that port, and this amount is rather above than below the average. If a vessel stocks £4 a day it is thought she is doing well, and a skipper's share does not generally exceed £1 per week, and if he make 7s. or 10s. more than that he is thought to be lucky.

According to Mr. Charles Hellyer, of Hull, the maximum earnings of a sailing trawler from that port clear of stock charges are £1,400 a year, while he thinks the fleet average £850.

He thinks an average year's work for a skipper not owning any of the vessel would be £110. The skipper takes eleven sixty-fourths of net stock, mate nine sixty-fourths, and third hand if by share, gets occasionally nine sixty-fourths but generally eight sixty-fourths or is paid by the week, the wages being about £1 per week and found by owner. The deck or fourth hand is generally hired as there are few apprentices now, and gets 18s. per week, while the cook's wages—he being the smallest—ranges from 10s. to 12s. per week, both of these are found by the owner. In addition to the shares and wages the crew have exclusive right to the fish livers, the proceeds from which are divided into four shares, the skipper, mate, and third hand getting a share each, the deck hand two thirds and the cook one third of a share.

According to the Duke of Edinburgh:

"The crews of the trawlers engaged in the North Sea are fed by the owners, and receive a certain rate of pay weekly, in addition to which they are paid a percentage of the amount realized by the sale of all fish caught."

This statement, that the crews of the North Sea trawlers are fed by the owners, is only partially correct, as has been shown, since the shares men pay a part of the grub bill. And it is also a fact that a portion of the crew are hired at least from some of the larger ports, and have no pecuniary interest in the catch. The statement he has made may apply to certain localities, as Yarmouth, for instance, but it is not generally applicable.

"The system of division on the Channel trawlers is somewhat different, namely:

		Shares
Owner receives	...	6
Master receives		1½
Two men each 1 share		2
		—
Total ...		7

The boys do not share in the catch.

Mr. Fox tells me that the crews of the Yarmouth trawlers are much by the week receiving, however, certain amounts of the stock resulting from the sale of the fish. The weekly wages paid at the present time to skipper and crew amount to the total of £18, equal to about $87. Besides this, three quarters of the net sum is divided among the crew, the skipper taking one and half shares—a bonus to keep his own among the other men. This is called a poundage, because it is a certain part of each pound earned by the vessel. It should be stated that, as the drifters (herring vessels) are at sea, the wages enumerated are in larger than quoted above, for the reason that the men are sought after by the skippers of the herring catchers. At such time it is often as much for the owners of trawlers to pay as much as £5 than $24 a week for the skipper and crew to keep the men.

The Yarmouth men are paid in gear and provisions over and paying all expenses.

The skippers and men are supplied as they can be obtained, as in New England. The men often more in demand for increased pay, and if a vessel is ready for sea and no crew to be had, frequent is a succeed in making the owners to pay large wages.

EFFECT OF BEAM TRAWLING ON THE ABUNDANCE OF FISH GROUNDS FREQUENTED BY BRITISH VESSELS.

Much has been said and written, pro and con, concerning the effect of beam trawling upon the abundance of fish. Among practical fishermen there appears to be a remarkable consensus of opinion on the subject. With few exceptions they believe that there has been a marked diminution of fish on all the grounds and rarely visited by beam trawlers, and not a few are ready to predict almost the entire destruction of many species which was a consequence of this fishing, so that were formerly rich feeding grounds for trawling, now being so poor, that are seldom visited. It is a somewhat remarkable fact that the earliest notice obtainable of this subject was the petition to Parliament 1376–77 quoted on page two of this report, speaks of the destruction of immature fish and the consequential evil effect on the fisheries that to result from the use of such apparatus. The same thing has been pointedly brought to the notice of the British Government, and a large mass of evidence has been submitted to establish this point, and urge as a reason for putting restrictions upon beam trawl fishing. The annual report of the London Fish Trade Association for 1888 calls attention to the report of the fish supply committee, dated August-November, 1881, and which, among other matter, contains the following:

"The first point which strikes us, and upon which stress should be laid, is the destruction of spawn and small of fish, and the taking of immature fish. The evidence proves conclusively that in quantities of immature fish are uselessly destroyed, and also that many of the ancient fishing-grounds have been and are greatly deteriorated and have ceased to be productive; and we are of opinion that the court should communicate with Her Majesty's Government, urging that legislative steps be promptly taken to remedy these evils.

On the other hand several eminent scientists have claimed that it is quite impossible for man to materially influence the supply of fish life in the ocean. And it is a singular fact that almost at the very time (winter of 1888-'89) when the Scotch fishermen, chiefly those engaged in line fishing, were testifying before a royal commission, and stating, with scarcely a dissenting voice, that the system of beam-trawl fishing was ruining the inshore grounds to such an extent as to make them almost worthless, fish of all kinds should be found off the Scottish coast in numbers not equaled for many years. Mr. J. J. Robertson Carr, writing under date of February 12, 1889, says:

Both trawler and line fisherman have had heavy catches of cod, ling, haddock, and flat fish; and as to size and quality, all are agreed that this season's fish are rarely surpassed.

The following dispatch, from the Edinburgh Scotsman of February 21, 1889, is corroborative of Mr. Carr's statement. Under the heading of "Remarkable Success of the Winter's Fishing on the Scottish Coasts," it says:

At the last meeting of the Scottish Fishery Board returns from the various districts were presented showing that unprecedented success had attended the prosecution of the winter fisheries on certain parts of the Scottish coasts. In the Eyemouth district no less than 92 tons of haddocks were caught in one week, the value of which was £1,400. The average earnings to round nearly £15 per boat; and during the season the total quantity of haddocks landed by all boats was computed at 924 tons, bringing to the fishermen something like £12,000. This it is estimated would give an average yield and value per boat probably exceeding that for the corresponding period of any previous year. The Montrose fishermen met with similar success, the haddock fishing in that district having been rarely if ever so remunerative. In one week some of the crews realized from £40 to £45 per boat. The enormous hauls occasioned for some time have not, however, been confined to haddocks. In the Anstruther district there were 12,365 crans of herrings landed in one week, part of which 4,000 telegrams were dispatched and sold fresh, 8 tons cured. At Wick alone were there landed in addition, a very remarkable haul of herrings, some large quantities of whitefish, comprising about 1,643 cod, and ling 1,200 saithe, 10 tons of plaice, 2 tons of haddocks, 2 tons of halibut, 4 cwt of hake, 1 cwt of soles, 200 skate, etc.

Though the above would seem to throw considerable doubt upon the correctness of statements which go to show the decrease in the abundance

Immense hauls are not uncommon; seven persons lost a boat.

ance of fish on trawling grounds, we nevertheless can not lose sight of the fact that the testimony of those best qualified to know positively the merits of this question is [illegible] of no value. The following extracts from a lecture delivered by Mr. Edward [illegible] (a salesman at Billingsgate, formerly a practical fisherman, and still a smack owner) at the Norwich Fisheries Exhibition in 188[illegible] will be of interest in this connection as showing the other side of the question:

"I am well aware there are those who will not admit of any falling off in the supply of trawl fish; but the old proverb, 'Facts are stubborn things,' is strictly applicable to this case, and I do not doubt that by adducing the plain incontrovertible facts without any distortion, I shall be able to prove that the answer just given by many is the perfectly correct one. For this purpose it will be necessary for me to go back for a few years from the present—twenty to twenty-five will suffice. At that period a first-class trawling vessel was not more than half the size of many of the splendid vessels of to-day, some of them from 50 to 80 tons, and working a beam nearly if not fully double the length; consequently the mouth of one of these nets will go over double as much ground as a net would twenty-five years back, and with what result? One of the small vessels with a net about half the size would at that period take, in nearly every case, as much fish in a week as one of these large vessels now obtains in a week, and the fish were much larger; in fact, the full-grown matured fish were so plentiful that the small fish such as taken now would at that time have been nearly valueless. The gentlemen present who have been engaged in the trawl fishing for so long a period will I have no doubt be able to corroborate my statements. I also wish to impress upon you my hearers that there are now fully five or six times the number of vessels employed in the deep-sea fisheries round our coasts than there were twenty-five years ago; yet with all this increase in vessels and the increased size of the net, we at the present time find, and have found for some time past, a very large falling off in this branch of the fisheries.

"Thirty-five years back there were from the port of Hull [illegible] vessels engaged in trawling; their combined tonnage was [illegible] tons, and their insurance value £6,000; but to-day there are 450 vessels, their tonnage 31,500 tons, and insurance value £[illegible].

"The surest index to the supply of fish is, and always will be, the quantity which is upon sale in the various markets, and the prices of the same. Twenty years ago soles were sold 12s. to 20s. a trunk, plaice and haddocks at 5s. per trunk, and all other kinds of trawl fish at equally low prices and within reach of the humblest homes of the land. As time has gone on so has the trawl fishing gone on [illegible] for the worse. That splendid and nutritious fish the sole is being swept out of our seas, is no more the cheap food of the poor and middle classes, but is nearly a luxury on the rich man's table, and is almost a rarity to some fishmongers' shops. During this last month I have sold trunks of soles at from £5 to £10, and plaice at from 15s to 21s per trunk, haddocks from 12s to 16s, and all other kinds of fish have been proportionately high.

"To what cause can we assign these high prices? Simply that the shortness of the supply of fish is out of all proportion to what it was for vessels twenty or twenty-five years back. If it were not so, we should find it be it strongly in favor of the purchaser; but with the large numbers of vessels of the finest class, and every means in our cause for the capture of fish, we have found the decrease in the catches has had such an effect on the advance in prices that the smack owner of to-day, in many cases, is quite unable to live by his industry; his vessel and gear, instead of being a source of profit, are a burden upon his hands. For the past few years I fear there are but few who have cleared their way, particularly trawlers. Not only in the price is the difference to be noticed but in the size; at the period of which I am speaking, twenty-five years ago the fish sent to the various markets of the kingdom were of a proper size, but such is not now the case. At the present time a very large proportion of the fish sent for sale to the various markets are but little more than small brood and fry, and ought not to be captured. This is not only the case of one particular description, but is applicable to every description of fish taken with either the trawl, drift, or seine and other nets I have before named. Take, for instance, the small plaice and haddocks from several parts; likewise let us look at the small immature fish sent for sale from all parts of the coast. The sole, which has acquired the designation among the buyers of 'slips' and 'tongues,' these tongues vary from 5 to 9 inches in length, and it must be borne in mind that I am speaking of the appearance of such fish in our markets not as unfrequent but as of daily occurrence. There are of these small immature fish as many in one box as would fill four to six boxes at least if they were allowed to grow twelve months longer. These small fish frequently fill only half or two thirds of a box, and are covered over with a few middle and large-sized fish. No person will for a moment contend that such small immature fish are fitted for the food of mankind. Why is it that these small fry are caught and the food of our increasing population destroyed?

"I will here mention some of the principal fishing-grounds, and I can say most emphatically that many of them are depopulated to such an extent that very few will pay a trawler to work them; others are becoming in a like state as rapidly as possible. There is not one of the fishing-grounds I will here name have the fish upon them there were a few years back. Rye Bay, the Diamond Ridge and Varne, the Falls Inner and Outer Gabbard, the Flats, Smiths Knoll, the Leman Shoals of the Hurn, Winterton Ridge, North Northeast Hole, Well Bank, Black Bank, Swart Bank, Botany Gut, Silver Pits, Southwest Pit, Northwest Pit, Clay Deep, Southwest Flat, West Shoal, Dogger Swish, Dogger Bank, East Rough, Inner Ground and Off Ground, Outer and

Inner Rough, on the coast of Jutland, Horn Reef, Borkum, Ameland and Texel Banks, also the Little and Great Fisher Bank, and the grounds off Penzance, Plymouth, Brixham, and Dartmouth.

Mr. Fox, like many others, believes the cause of this depletion, is due, in a great measure, to the smallness of the mesh in the cod end of the trawls. This fact is so well recognized by many trawl fishermen that it has been mentioned in a previous chapter. Various devices have been brought forth to insure the escape of immature fish.

Just what will be the final result of beam trawling on the supply of fish it is now difficult to say, time alone can tell. While, however, it may be conceded that many who are in good positions to judge accurately have grave apprehensions of the future, it goes without saying that the fisherman who depends on his work to support himself and family can not afford to look beyond the present, but must use his utmost endeavors to catch all the fish he can, since it is for that purpose he ventures forth to brave the perils which always surround him.

K.—A CRUISE ON A BRITISH NORTH SEA TRAWLER.

Previous to my departure from the United States to attend, on the staff of Prof. G. Brown Goode, the International Fishery Exhibition held at Berlin, Germany, in 1880, I was instructed by Prof. Spencer F. Baird, United States Commissioner of Fish and Fisheries, to make one or more cruises on a first-class beam trawler, if it was found practicable to do so. The object in view was that a practical study of the beam trawl fishery might be made, and as much information gathered of its details as would enable me to prepare a report sufficiently full and explicit to convey to American fishermen a comprehensive idea of the apparatus used and the methods of fishing. Professor Baird, being fully cognizant of the importance of the beam trawl fisheries of Europe, and having in mind the enormous extent of the fishing grounds to which citizens of the United States have access, deemed it desirable that this should be done. The result of my studies of the British beam trawl fishery, then and subsequently, has been given in the preceding pages, to which the following account of a cruise in a Grimsby trawler may perhaps be appropriately added.

Leaving Berlin on the evening of June 20, 1880, with Professor Goode and his private secretary, Mr. Julius E. Rockwell, we reached Flushing the following evening, and arrived in London on the 22d. On the next day after our arrival, Professor Goode and myself met Mr. Spencer Walpole, now lieutenant-governor of the Isle of Man, but then inspector of British salmon fisheries, who very kindly gave us the benefit of his knowledge and advice in regard to the best locality to visit in order to gain definite information of the beam trawl fishery. This he decided to be Grimsby, at the mouth of the Humber River, and which is one of the most important fishing stations in Great Britain. He also provided me with a letter of introduction to Mr. Harrison Mudd, a gentleman largely interested in the fisheries of Grimsby, and who held the official position of town counselor of that port.

Passage for New York had been provisionally taken for our party on the North German Lloyds steamship *Nectar*, which was booked to sail from Southampton July 6, and it was thought that if I could get away on a trawler within a day or two there would be ample time to make a short cruise—long enough to get an idea of the fishery—and for me to reach Southampton soon enough to join the rest of our party on the *Nectar*, though this was only a secondary consideration which was not to interfere at all with my trip. Accordingly I left London next morning (June 24) and reached Grimsby the same day. After some delay I had the gratification of meeting with Mr. Mudd, who having been made aware of the object of my visit, assured me in the kindest manner that he would aid me all he could in procuring a chance to go out on a trawler. It is proper that acknowledgment should be made here of the obligation I am under to this gentleman who interested himself to get me a berth on a good vessel, and to whose courtesy I am much indebted for any success which may have been obtained in gaining a knowledge of the beam trawl fishery.

No trawlers were sailing that evening on which Mr. Mudd thought I ought to go, but he believed it probable some might go out the following day. He thought it would not be advisable—as my time was so limited—for me to go out on a single hatter? which might be gone two or three weeks; neither would he advise that a cruise should be made on a cutter bound to the ... steamer fleet, which at that time was working off the German coast some 400 miles or more distant from Grimsby, since with the prevailing light winds the vessel might be nearly a week in reaching the fishing ground and the fleet with which she worked. The best chance for me, it was considered, would be to go out on a smack that was to join one of the small cutter fleets on the Dogger Bank, which would probably be reached in twenty-four hours with favorable winds; thus I might have several days on the fishing ground, observe the method of working the beam trawl etc., and return by another vessel in time to reach Southampton and sail on the *Nectar*. The smack *Welfare and Ida* was fitting out to join one of the cutter fleets. Mr. Mudd thought she would sail the next day, and he assured me I could have a chance on her whenever she went to sea. I learned however on the following day, which was Friday, June 25) that the *Welfare and Ida* would not sail before the Monday following, because of the accidental sinking of her boat in the dock, by which this trip two of her crew were nearly drowned and rendered quite unfit, for a day or two to go to sea. As no other smacks were sailing to the cutter fleets before Monday, either from Grimsby or Hull—as was ascertained later—there was nothing to do but to wait.

In the interim there was an opportunity to note the various phases

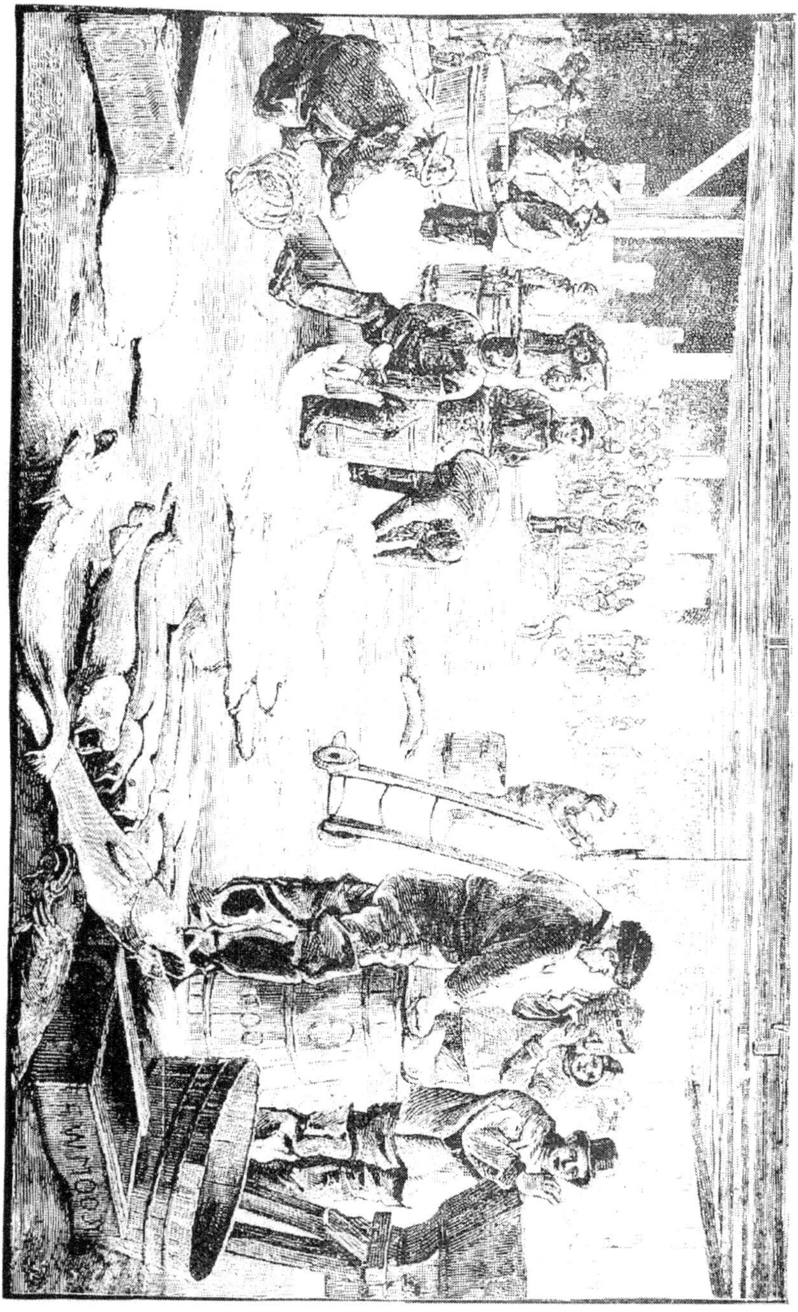

GRIMSBY FISH MARKET: RECEIVING, SELLING, AND PACKING FISH.

of the fish trade is conducted at Grimsby, who differs considerably from the methods adopted in the United States. In a previous paragraph the statement has been made that Grimsby had little importance as a fishing port previous to 1858, when her trawling vessels first introduced. And for many years previous to 1848 the harbor was practically closed to navigation by the accumulation of mud and sand at its mouth, which in the reign of Charles I became so increased, that the smaller fishing vessels could with difficulty approach the town. At present it possesses several large docks two of which are exclusively devoted to the fisheries and known as the cod and ice fish docks. These have a total area of 25 acres with market attached on what is locally known as the pontoon, 1,000 feet in length on one side of which the smacks lie and discharge their cargoes while on the other side stand the railway cars or fish vans upon which are sent away to billingsgate and other markets the fish that are constantly arriving. These facilities for receiving, packing, and shipping fish are as excellent as they are unique and have resulted in an increase of the fish trade of Grimsby from between 1,000 and 3,000 tons in 1858 to over 75,000 tons in 1882 while it is claimed that the population has about trebled itself, and the fleet increased from a few small smacks to about eight hundred sail of the finest fishing vessels in Great Britain.

The following statements relative to the fish trade of the port are vouched for by three of the largest firms in Grimsby, and no doubt may be accepted as correct.

That Grimsby is unquestionably the largest and most promising fishing port in the kingdom may be seen by the following facts. In the year 1853 there were but 12 fishing vessels in this port and no facilities for the trade whatever. At the present time there are 825 vessels belonging to the port solely engaged in fishing, with an estimated registered tonnage of 42,000 valued at £725,000 carrying 1,110 men and boys. Besides the above the port is frequently visited by many Dutch and other fishing vessels for the sale of their cargoes. There are 50,000 tons of ice imported annually, which is not only used by the smacks at sea but for packing in the market, and is sent in various forms to all parts of the kingdom.

The railway company has expended nearly half a million sterling in the making of docks and otherwise providing for the fishery trade and are still extending and ever increasing.

From 2,000 to 30,000 codfish, besides large quantities of other fish, are kept ready for sale in boxes in the fish ice dock. The advantages offered to the trade of Grimsby over other markets are found in the great variety, the constant supply, the means of storing fish alive, the many cutting houses, the care and facilities given by the railway company, the superior quality by the adoption of steam trawlers and smacks, and the ready and cheap supply of ice.

Extensive business is now carried on with the far north of Scotland,

Dublin, Belfast, Carmarthen, Plymouth, Torquay, Hastings, Brighton, the Isle of Wight, Rotterdam, Hamburg, and Paris."

FIG. 23. ICE MILL USED BY FISH PACKERS.

As the tide approaches nearly to its full, the dock gates are opened, which is a signal for a busy and exciting scene. All is hurry and bustle on board of the smacks that are ready for sea, and which are rapidly got under way and either sail or are towed out to sea through one of the entrances to the "fish dock," while through the other gate may be seen entering, one after the other, the vessels which have been hovering just outside—waiting for the rising tide—and whose signals and numbers have communicated to those on shore the welcome news of their arrival. Smacks from the "cutter" and "bulking" fleets, "single-boaters," steam carriers from the "steamer" fleets, long-liners, hand-liners, freighters from Norway, some with lobsters others with fresh mackerel; on they come, shooting through the narrow entrance, to quickly find their berths in dock. On the pier-heads are gathered scores of men, and occasionally women and children—if the day be fine—some waving a sainte and wishing "good luck" to their departing friends, while others stand ready to give a greeting of welcome to the hardy fishermen returning, perhaps, from an absence of months. As the smacks arrive no time is lost in getting them into their respective berths, and if there be a considerable number they haul in and make fast, head on, to the "pontoon," upon which the cargoes are discharged with as little delay as possible. As the fish are taken out they are sorted according to their grades or the condition in which they arrive. For instance, the fish taken alive from the well of a smack, having first been knocked on the head to kill them, are laid out in rows according to their species,

or grade, while the "boxed" fish from the trawling fleets are sold
another lot. No busier scene can be imagined than transpires here e_
day, and considering the quantities of fish displayed one can not _
being occasionally surprised at the prices they sell for. All fish
disposed of by a number of salesmen, each of whom is empowere_
contract to sell the catch of a certain number of smacks, he receivi_
percentage on the sales for his services. Cod are sold by the score (_
is, 20 fish), and these, with halibut and ling, are knocked off to the h_
est bidder; trawled fish are, however, generally sold at Dutch auct_
which is thus described by Holdsworth:

"A lot of turbot, perhaps, is to be sold; the salesman's bell is _
and the stentorian voice of the auctioneer is heard calling out, '_
then, turbot buyers, turbot buyers, turbot buyers, come along, ye
bot buyers.' A knot of people collects and the salesman descants _
few words on the quality of the fish; a price is named, no one respo_

Fig. 24. Loading fish vans.

or indeed is expected to do so, for it begins too high for any deali_
it comes down by degrees until a nod from one of the crowd closes
transaction, and the sale is booked. Then calls may be made for '_
buyers,' 'plaice buyers,' 'ling buyers,' or 'cod buyers,' and the wo_
rapidly got through, for there is no time to be wasted over indivi_
lots where they are so many to be sold, packed, and sent away as _
as possible."

They are packed with ice in crates, barrels, and in box cars, spec_
designed for the purpose, and shipped by swift running trains to _
various markets they are consigned to.

All arrangements for the cruise having previously been made, I went on board the *Willie and Ada*, Capt. Henry Tidder, on Monday morning, June 28, and at 9 o'clock a. m., soon after the dock gates were opened, our smack was shoved out beyond the pier heads, all sail was set, and with a moderate southwest breeze and fine weather we left the Humber's mouth, passed Spurn Point, and headed away from the land toward that famous fishing ground of the North Sea, the Dogger Bank, where we expected to meet with the fleet we were to join, and where our fishing operations were to be carried on. The *Willie and Ada* was 73.68 tons register, ketch or "dandy" rigged, and manned by a crew of five, three of whom were men, the other two—the "fourth" hand or deck hand and cook—being boys of respectively seventeen and fourteen years of age.* The crew slept and ate in the cabin, which, considering the number to be accommodated, was roomy and comfortable, being painted and grained, but differing from the cabins of modern American fishing schooners in being under deck, and in some details of arrangement.

The wind died entirely away during the afternoon, and we lay becalmed until evening, when a moderate breeze again sprang up from the southwest. The day was fine throughout, and was spent by me in gathering information concerning the construction of the beam trawl, the peculiarities of the vessel—so far as speed, ability in a gale, etc., were concerned—and in making sketches.

Tuesday, June 29.—The wind continued moderate during the night, but, as it was fair, the vessel slipped along easily through the water, which was so smooth that scarcely any motion could be noticed, unless one glanced over the side and saw the scintillating phosphorescent sparkle of the sea go by as we glided through it. At 5 a. m. the captain sounded and "struck the rough" on the Dogger Bank. Two hours later we spoke a homeward-bound cutter. Our skipper inquired the whereabouts of "Biscomb's lot," meaning the fleet we were to join, of which a captain by the name of Biscomb was "admiral." He was told that they were some three hours' sail—15 or 16 miles—distant in the direction we had been going. We then resumed our course, and at 9 o'clock a. m. the captain, who had been aloft at the masthead looking out for "Biscomb's lot," came on deck and reported seeing two fleets nearly ahead. We steered for the nearest fleet, which, however, did not prove to be the one we were in search of, but the skipper of one of the smacks which we hailed pointed to leeward and said: "That's Biscomb's lot, down there, I think." This proved to be the case, and soon after the order was given to our crew to "Get up the trawl bridles and shackle them on," our skipper remarking at the same time, "They have their gear down, and I don't know how long it's been out." As

*Details [illegible] recorded some many facts that were [illegible] [illegible] these notes have been given elsewhere, and also because more or less of [illegible] is shown in the illustrations.

board was hauling, and the crew tumbled out of their bunks, hurriedly pulled on their heavy leather boots, and, jamming their hats or sou'westers on their heads, ran on deck and began to get up the trawl.[1] The process was an interesting study for me, as I then saw it for the first time. I assisted in the work, heaving on the capstan and helping the skipper to get the dandy bridle in and the after end of the trawl beam up to the vessel's stern.

We had been towing over ground which was more or less rocky, and which is known to the fishermen by the technical name of "The Rough," so that when they are fishing on such bottom, which they sometimes do in summer because fish are more abundant there than elsewhere, they call it "working The Rough." As a result of our "working The Rough" on this occasion the trawl had been badly torn, which mishap was first announced while the net was being gathered in, the second hand exclaiming, in a somewhat disheartened voice, "She's all gone to smithereens." The mishap was not quite so bad, however, as was at first expected, and about 300 pounds of fish still remained in the cod end, which was hoisted on board and the catch let out on deck. In this small lot there were many varieties,[2] chief among which were turbot, sole, lemon sole, which is a different species from the common sole (*Solea solea*), plaice, cod, hake, ling, gurnard, goosefish or monkfish (*Lophius*), besides a large number of starfishes, anemones, sea corn (eggs of whelks), and sea pens, which, together with small rocks and more or less sea grass and shells, made up a very interesting collection, though it was not "fishy" enough to have any special merit or attraction for the smack's crew.

As soon as the trawl was emptied of its contents the stay-foresail was hoisted and the vessel filled away by the wind, the fourth hand took the helm and was ordered to "keep her along after the fleet," which was then to windward of our vessel working up for a new berth. (See fig. 75.) The skipper, second, and third hands went to work to mend the net, but when this job was well advanced the mending was continued by the two former, while the third hand was ordered to "box the fish," which order implied that he should dress and pack in boxes such as were marketable (about two-thirds of the lot) and throw the remainder overboard. In this instance, however, only the hake, turbot, cod, and haddock were dressed—that is, eviscerated; the others were simply washed before being packed, but were not gutted.

In the meantime our diminutive cook was actively employed in the cabin preparing supper, which all seemed glad to partake of, the ap-

[1] The [illegible] trawl heaving up [illegible] on this occasion [illegible] the paragraph "Some methods of fishing," page 12 of this report.

[2] Besides [illegible] other species of fish were taken [illegible] which may [illegible] fishes [illegible]

petites of the crew having been sharpened somewhat by the vigorous exercise of heaving up the trawl.

Having worked to windward for about two or three hours, the trawl was shot again at 8 p. m. This time the vessel was on the starboard tack and the trawl was "shot around the stern." This was a new feature of the business, and, as the weather was fine, an excellent opportunity was afforded to note all the details. After the trawl was down the watch was set and the rest turned in.

Fig. 25. Working up for a breeze.

Wednesday, June 30.—All hands were called out to heave up the gear at 1 o'clock a. m. I had staid up late the previous evening to gain some additional information about trawling, and to watch the fleet as the vessels worked slowly along, the bright lights of the smacks being plainly discernible in the hazy darkness of the summer's night, as the vessels rose and fell in the long undulating swell of the North Sea. Therefore, though it was bright sunlight at the time the admiral signaled to "haul trawls," I was first wakened by the skipper shouting to the tired and sleepy third hand: "You Tom! You Tom! come, rouse out here and haul!" Out we tumbled and on deck, where the cranks were already shipped on the capstan; the hatch off, and down in the hold, ready to coil away the trawl-warp, was the small boy, who not only officiates in the capacity of cook but must always be promptly on hand to assist wherever his services are required. All hands fell to with a will, the skipper racked the vessel back and forth—working up over the gear—while the clink, clink, clink of the capstan told that the trawl warp was being rapidly got on board.

The catch on this occasion did not exceed over 200 pounds weight of marketable fish, though nearly everything was saved, including skate, dabs, and catfish. As in this case, however, the net had not been torn, the skipper offered, as a reasonable explanation of the small catch, the statement that there was little or no wind during much of the past night, consequently the vessel could not tow the trawl fast enough over the bottom to catch any fish—in fact for much of the time we had been doing little else than drifting with the tide in a calm. In the morning the wind breezed up quite briskly, and continued fresh throughout the day.

After the trawl was up all sail was set and the smack worked to windward to join the rest of the fleet, which had not drifted quite so much to leeward during the night. Meanwhile, the fish were "boxed," and it was announced that one of the smacks which had her "cargo done fixing, would leave the fleet this morning for home, after the catch of the other vessels for the previous day and night had been put on board of her.

It is difficult to imagine a more lively and inspiriting nautical scene than was presented on this summer's morning by the little fleet to which our cutter belonged, and the center of which was the homeward-bound craft, lying to with net flag flying. All around her were collected the other vessels of the fleet, standing back and forth under all sail, their heavy square-headed gaff topsails aloft to catch the breeze, boats passing to and fro going to the cutter—to take their fish, to send letters, etc. visiting other vessels of the fleet recently out from the land (one of which was our smack), to hear the news from home, obtain letters and secure supplies that had been sent to them. The picturesque tanned sails glowing blood-red in the sunlight, the shouting back and forth between the crews of the different vessels as they came within hail, were additional interesting characteristics of the scene.

On our own vessel the boat had been launched stern foremost over the lee side. As soon as she struck the water one man sprang into her, and to him were passed the two "trunks" of fish we had caught, these being dropped or roughly stowed in the middle of the boat. A second man then jumped into the boat, and when the proper time arrived she was cast off and pulled away for the carrier smack to discharge the fish. "Boarding the fish," as it is called, on this occasion, when the sea was smooth and only a moderate breeze blowing, was every game affair compared with such work when the weather is rough. Many wonderful tales are told by the fishermen of hairbreadth escapes from drowning while engaged in transporting their fish from their vessels to the carrier, and considering that this work is done in almost all kinds of weather, one can easily believe that it is extremely hazardous, to say the least.

The catch being small on this occasion the boats were soon finished, the crews returned to their respective vessels, the admiral showed to signal for starting, and as the fleet stood off close hauled for the fishing ground their companion, the homeward bound cutter set sail and filled away for Grimsby.

I sent a letter by her to Professor Goode in London, and decided to stay out until the next cutter went in.

The fleet kept under full sail, working to windward about two hours when at 10 o'clock a. m. the trawls were shot where the ground was rather rocky.

After towing about an hour our trawl caught hard of the bottom, as is to stop the vessel entirely. We have it up and found it had swept an old anchor weighing about 140 pounds that was still hanging to the net, which had been so badly torn by it that all the fish, if there were any in the trawl, had made their escape. This was rather discouraging to the crew, the members of which, however, took the matter rather coolly, and with far less grumbling than one might naturally expect they pulled in the net and began to mend it. As soon as the repairs were completed the trawl was put out again, but misfortune again awaited us, for in about an hour and a half it got fastened to the bottom and it was necessary to heave it up. By this time several other vessels of the fleet were seen in the same predicament, and perhaps on the principle that misery loves company, our crew seemed to derive a certain sort of grim satisfaction from the fact that they were not the only ones having ill luck, and it was thought that when so many of the fleet met with this mishap the admiral would lose faith in working "The Rough."

When it was up we found the trawl badly split; indeed, in this instance it would have been more suggestive to say it was all gone in so many ends, and five or six plaice that were jammed in the pocket constituted its entire contents. The skipper scowled and then loud turned to again to repair damages, and, as the rest of the fleet have no their gear about the same time, we all filled away and stood along by the wind until 8 p. m. when in obedience to the admiral's signal the trawl was shot in 20 fathoms. We had previously fished in from 18 to 21 fathoms, and for the most part as has been indicated on rough ground.

Capt. Fidder believes that little can be done working The Rough even where fish are comparatively plenty, since the gear is liable to much damage and may possibly be rendered entirely useless. Spare trawl nets, beams, heads, etc., are carried on the smacks to replace losses which may occur, but it is evident that should these be much in even all the spare gear may be destroyed and the vessel compelled to leave the ground and go in for more. This rarely happens so far as could be learned.

The day was spent by me, like its predecessors on this trip, in taking notes and making sketches, varied by assisting the men to heave in the gear, and steering, when it was necessary for all the others to be at work.

Thursday, July 1.—At 3.15 a. m. the watch came below, called the skipper, and told him that the ground was hauling. As the skipper tumbled out of his berth he gave a quick glance around to see if all of the crew were up. His eye rested on the third hand, who, having been on watch all the first part of the night, was naturally very sleepy, and was still slumbering in profound unconsciousness of the admiral's order. But the sleeping man was quickly brought to a realizing sense of the situation, and swarmed out of his berth in obedience to the order of the skipper, who shouted in stentorian tones: "Now Tom, here, rouse out here and haul the trawl." All hands were on deck and at work in a remarkably brief space of time. No minutes are wasted in preparing for the day's duties; that is to say, no stopping to wash, not the faintest attempt at personal cleanliness, even the boy cook is begrimed with coal dust smoke, and soot; it is evident that little is thought of refinement even such as may be obtained from a dip in a bucket of salt water. The intention is *to catch fish*, and the toil and hardship incident to this vocation, for necessity that always exists for tumbling out—all standing—and rushing on deck, serves to make these men—as well as all other fishermen the world over—rather indifferent while fishing, to the simplest forms of neatness, which to people on land is considered indispensable.

When in obedience to the call to work, as on this occasion the hull wakened fisherman springs out of his bunk to the cabin floor, he realizes first of all the necessity of getting on deck with the least possible delay; therefore, with eyes still half closed, he gropes for his boots, pulls them on, snatches his hat from some convenient place where it has been put, and runs it on his head. Thus, if the weather be fine completes his equipment, but if it is stormy oil clothes are also donned. In either case the least possible time must be occupied, and frequently the men are not fairly awake until after they reach the deck.

When the end of the trawl warp was inside the roller, the skipper looked over the vessel's side and exclaimed: "She's capsized again," meaning that the trawl was upset, which he could easily tell by the bridles being crossed.

It was explained by the skipper, in answer to my inquiry, that the capsize was caused by the vessel, when working up to the gear, bringing the warp taut in the opposite direction from which the trawl was being towed over the bottom. This turned the trawl over on its back, bringing the beam underneath and a twist in the bridles; since the foot warp end of the beam is up, the position on the roller being told is soon as the upper ends of the bridles are in. The dandy bridle was cast off the trawl warp, and a stopper put on the after bridle, which was then unshuckled. By passing the ends of these around the forward bridle, outside of the smacks, and the turns were taken out so that they led clear.

The dandy bridle was then made fast on the port side of the vessel, and led to the dandy wince; when the bridle was set taut, the trawl-beam turned end for end, and swung at its proper position, which it was hove up to the usual way.

The catch of fish was found this morning, mounting only a trunks of plaice, one trunk of mixed fish—cod, skate, &c.—a conger eel—and one or two turbot in number, little over a 300 weight in all. The fishermen agreed in saying that the catch on trips is unusually light, though at this season fish are generally in this region. They tell of catching 4,000 and 5,000 pounds a day, and mention instances when as many as 10,000 pounds are taken at a single haul, the species captured on these occasions chiefly haddock.

When the trawl was up and made sail—that is got under way, stood along a short distance to join the rest of the fleet now around the smack *Soberty*, which was the next to sail for Co. The morning's catch of the fleet was put on board, her, and she that she would sail the next day for market, providing fish enough taken in the mean time to complete her cargo.

There was a brisk northerly breeze in the morning, with fog, but the wind moderated considerably during the forenoon, and it calming about 9 a.m.

At 11 a.m. we shot the trawl around the stern in 19 fathoms of and towed away to the westward on the starboard tack. Nothing got on board again, and about 200 pounds of fish were in the trawl, most of which were plaice.

We then stood along, by the wind on the starboard tack, about northwest until 8 p.m. when the trawl was shot for the the vessel still heading westerly. On this occasion the trawl taken around the smack's bow instead of being hauled under the tom, as it formerly had been. This was done to prevent it from chafed, also that it might be in a position to bring the vessel to in case we met with other smacks during the night towing posite direction.

Friday, July 2.—A little after midnight—about 12:15 a.m.—awakened to see the vessel veer around while towing, the usual object of this manoeuvre is generally to change the tack with the of the tide, and thereby tow the trawl back nearly over the same it passed across during the first of the night. Or, perhaps on occasion it is done to keep clear of rough bottom, which the lead warning of. A smack can of course be tacked around with the out, as has been mentioned, and this can be done quicker, and then to wear; but unless the conditions are favorable, too much le hable to be upset.

The manner of setting the trawl has been described in the Methods of Fishing.

Bull. U. S. F. C. 87——25

There was a brisk westerly breeze in the morning with fine clear weather, but later in the day the wind moderated slightly and there were light showers of rain in the evening

The trawl was landed at 5 a. m. and though it was torn considerably there were about 1,200 pounds of fish in the cod. These were chiefly small haddock, such as the New England fishermen call "scrod" haddock. According to the skipper, we struck The Rough about half an hour before we began to heave up the trawl, which accounted for its being torn.

Most of the vessels in our fleet got fair catches of fish this morning, compared with what they had previously taken, and not a few of them had their nets torn. After the trawls were up, and while the crews were busy dressing and boxing the fish and repairing damages to the gear the fleet filled away and beat it to windward to regain the position where they began fishing last evening. The catch was not sufficiently large to complete the cargo of the *Sobraty* and consequently she did not start for market to-day. But I concluded, however, to change my quarters and when the boat left the *Willie and Ida* to transfer the morning's catch of fish I went in her on board of the *Sobraty* where I was welcomed by the captain and crew, and where I staid for the remainder of my cruise.

It was an interesting sight to witness from this point of view—on board of the cutter—the various phases of boarding the fish which have been alluded to elsewhere. Along the lee side of the *Sobraty* were crowded the boats of the fleet, the crew of some of them actively engaged in getting their fish on deck, upon which was gathered a group of hardy fishermen belonging to the other vessels and who now their fish were on board and their boats dropped astern, were inter changing news, chaffing the newcomers and apparently enjoying this break in the monotony of their lives on board their own vessels.

The crew of the cutter which takes the fish in generally have to stow the boxes below and ice them, putting down alternate layers of trunks of fish and ice, the latter being ground fine in a mill which each smack of the fleet is provided with. Sometimes the cutter's crew receive as sistance from the men belonging to the other vessels who, after they have discharged their boats and deposited their bulls of lading in the companion hold, are asked to get the trunks below deck. When, however, all the vessels in a cutter fleet are sharing alike, each receiving an equal portion of the catch, no tallies are put on the trunks of fish and no bulls of lading are needed.

At 1:30 p. m. the admiral signaled to "shoot the gear" and accord ingly the trawl was put out. But it got caught upon the bottom soon after it was down and we had to heave it up and repair the damage which the net had sustained. As this took some time it was decided by our skipper that it would scarcely pay to make another shot during the afternoon, and as several other smacks met with a similar mishap, and none of them put out their gear after repairing it, they all gathered around a vessel just out from home, and the skippers went on board of her to learn the news and inquire for letters. As our captain was going, too, I joined him and spent two or three hours very pleasantly, learned some new facts about beam-trawling, and was gratified to find the fishermen communicative and intelligent, many of them possessing a comprehensive knowledge of the business in which they were engaged, and some having considerable general information.

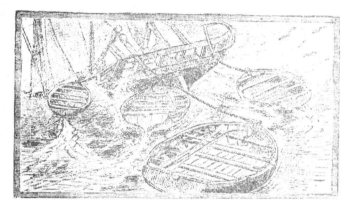

Fig. 26. VISITING.

I did some sketching to-day, but, owing to the prevalence of rainy weather since the cruise began, there have been few opportunities for securing sketches.

Saturday, July 5.—There was a fresh southwest breeze in the morning—a head wind for Grimsby, which materially decreased my chances of reaching Southampton to join the *Neckar.*

We began to heave up the trawl at 2.30 a. m., and at 5 o'clock it was alongside. About 800 to 1,000 pounds of fish were taken on this haul. After the trawl was up the smack filled away, and stood along to the westward, by the wind, with the rest of the fleet in company, until the fish were ready to put on board the *Sobriety,* when we hove to and waited for the morning's catch to be "boarded."

Several of the skippers, among whom was Captain Tidder, came aboard the *Sobriety* to bid me good bye, and to wish me a safe and speedy passage home. From all of these men I received uniform kindness and courtesy, while they have shown a willingness to give me all the information possible concerning their vocation.

As soon as the fish were all aboard our guests took their leave, our smack filled away, all sail but the jib-topsail was set, and we headed along about west by south, close-hauled on the port tack. When the fish were all below and iced the bobstay was hooked on and hove taut, and the photopsail set. This was at 11 p.m., at which time the wind was moderating, and it gradually decreased until it finally fell calm in the evening.

Sunday, July 4.—Began with light northerly breeze and drizzling rain. Wind increased at 4 a.m. to a fresh breeze, and after 11 a.m. it blew strong and squally.

At 10 a.m. we made the land a short distance north of Flamborough Head, which is 40 miles from Grimsby, and at 11 o'clock we passed Spurn Point. After rounding the point we took in the gaff topsails and big jib, set the small jib, and took a reef in the mainsail and mizzen, thus putting the vessel under easy sail to wait for the rising tide to reach its full. No vessel can enter the Grimsby docks until the signal is hoisted—an hour or so before high water—which, on this occasion was displayed a little before 2 p.m.

In the meantime we lay by off the harbor's mouth slowly reaching back and forth in company with several other inward bound vessels. Shortly after the signal was run up we shot into the dock, and the *Solarity* soon lay securely moored in her berth, ready to discharge on the following morning.

Immediately sent a telegram to Professor Goode, acquainting him with my arrival at Grimsby, and stating the hour when I should be in London on the following day.

In the evening I called on Mr. Mudd and informed him of my return and of the success which had attended the cruise.

Monday, July 5.—I reached London at noon, and joined Professor Goode; the same evening we arrived at Southampton in ample time to secure our berths on the *Nectar*, which was expected the following day.

II.—NOTES ON THE BEAM-TRAWL FISHERY OF CONTINENTAL EUROPE

A.—FRANCE

Though beam-trawling is prosecuted to a considerable extent by the French, this fishery has not assumed in France anything like the important proportions which it has attained in Great Britain. No statistics are available showing to what extent the beam-trawl fishery has been carried on in France; but when it is stated, on the authority of Mons. A. Duchochois, of Boulogne, that only twenty-five sailing trawlers go out from that important fishing port, and that France has no steam trawlers, some idea may be gained of the status of this fishery.

1.—FISHING-GROUNDS

The fishing-grounds on the North Sea and the English Channel are visited by the French trawlers in common with the English, though it is probable the former keep nearer the continental coast than the English do.

TRAWLERS IN THE FISH-DOCK AT GRIMSBY.

VESSELS.

Smacks are used for beam trawling, these carry crews of eight men each. Some of them are ketch-rigged, but others are cutter-rigged carrying only a single mast.

APPARATUS.

The beam trawls used by the French have the same general features as those employed by the English which have been fully described.

* In the French trawls the net is very much shorter in proportion to the length of the beam; it tapers regularly to the end, has no distinct cod, as in the English nets, and the rubbing pieces extend across the under side of the trawl for some distance from the end, which is specially protected from chafing by having a stout hide under each.

The ground rope is sometimes weighted with chain that is fastened to it in festoons similar to the plan adopted in Belgium fisheries.

The same pattern of head iron that is used by the English is also, I am informed, now most generally adopted by French fishermen. At the time Holdsworth wrote, other forms were in favor in France to considerable extent, though he mentions that even there the Brixham pattern was used.

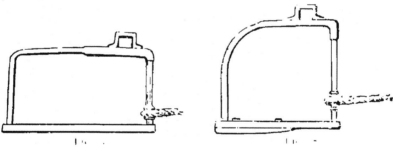

FRENCH TRAWL IRONS. (After Holdsworth.)

Concerning these peculiar forms of trawl heads he states as follows:

Among other varieties of trawl head may be mentioned those we have found used by some of the French trawlers, and the notice that feature in them is that the beam is placed so much in the front of the head is to require the tow rope to be fixed very low to prevent the fore part of the shoe burying itself in the ground. This is further guarded against in one variety, see fig. 27, by the additional length of the frame behind the beam. There appears to be a want of balance in these French irons which is not the case with those used by our own fishermen. No doubt there is some degree of fancy in the shapes adopted, but the English irons strike one as better adapted for their work, and the Brixham pattern is now being much used by the French trawlers. By means of these irons the trawl beam is kept nearly a foot above the ground, so that it neither touches nor causes any disturbance of the bottom whatever. Its sole use is to extend the mouth of the net, and if it were to touch the ground, as many persons believe it does, it would, undoubtedly, frighten away the fish and prevent their going into the net."

3. METHODS OF FISHING

The methods of fishing, so far as shooting and hauling the trawl are concerned, are essentially the same, according to M. Duchochois, as those adopted by English fishermen.

B. BELGIUM

According to M. Jules Le Lorrain there are about 222 vessels employed in the beam-trawl fisheries from Belgium, 170 of these sailing from Ostend and the remaining 52 from Heyst and Blankenberghe. There are also 22 small boats commonly called "sloops," engaged in this fishery on the Belgian coast. The foregoing will give an idea of the importance of the trawl fishery of Belgium, though it should be stated that some of the vessels do not, like the English, pursue this business throughout the year, but frequently engage in other branches of the fisheries.

1. FISHING GROUNDS

The fishing grounds resorted to are essentially the same as those upon which the English pursue their work in the North Sea.

2. VESSELS

The vessels employed in beam-trawling from Belgium are of two classes. The larger and more important type so closely resembles the English ketch-rigged trawler that the description given of the latter will apply as well to the Belgian smack, which differs from the other chiefly in having less rake to her stern-post and, perhaps, in a less elaborate equipment for working the gear. A capstan exhibited in the Belgian section at London was of the old-fashioned type, and as this was intended to represent the kind used for heaving up beam-trawls, it is evidently far less effective than the improved and powerful capstans carried on English trawlers.

The other class of Belgian trawlers are large, open, clinker-built boats very wide, with round bilge and flat bottom. They have a peculiar lug rig, average about 20 tons, and like the *bomschuiten* of Holland, are specially designed for fishing from a coast where harbors are not easily accessible.

[Documents relating to inquiries.]
The information used in the narrative of the Belgian beam-trawl fisheries is based partly upon a study of models of vessels and articles of apparatus exhibited at the International Fisheries Exposition, London, 1883, and partly upon information very kindly furnished by M. Jules Le Lorrain of Belgium.

The vessels sailing from Ostend carry each six men in a crew, while four men is the average crew on the Heyst and Blankenberghe trawlers.*

APPARATUS.

In most essential particulars the trawls used on the larger class of Belgian trawlers are constructed on the same general plan as those employed by the English.

There are some differences, however, in details, as may be gathered from the following description of a trawl exhibited in the Belgian section at London.

The foot of this net was first hung to a small hemp rope, about the size of ordinary nine-thread ratline stuff. This small rope is seized at intervals of six inches, to a larger hemp rope—about $1\frac{3}{4}$ inches in circumference—and the latter is fastened, by galvanized iron wire seizings, to the foot rope proper, which is $4\frac{3}{4}$-inch manila. Attached to

Fig. 29. Foot of Belgian trawl.

the ground rope by stout iron rings, are festoons or loops of chain, the rings being 6 inches apart and there being five or six links of chain in each loop. Fig. 29 is a section of the foot of a Belgian trawl, and shows this peculiarity of construction. This chain attachment is for the purpose of making the ground rope "bite" the bottom—that is, dig into it so as to disturb any flat fish, like soles, for instance, that cling close to the ground and partially bury themselves. One would think, however, that this plan might be objectionable, because if the ground rope should be caught up on rough bottom it seems probable that the trawl warp would part before the chain, and consequently the whole gear would be lost.

The Belgian trawl head (Fig. 30) has very nearly the same shape as the head irons used by the Hull and Grimsby fishermen, differing chiefly from the latter in the after part of the curve, from the beam to the shoe, being of round iron instead of flat, and in having the eye for the ground rope to bend into inside of the lower after corner instead of forming a

* Since the above was written steam trawlers have been successfully introduced in the Belgian fishery.

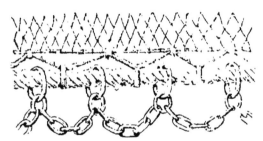

projecting out behind as in the English trawl head referred to, though in this respect it is similar to the English "Barking pattern."

The end of the beam projects several inches beyond the socket and is held in place by a stout iron key. Iron wedges are not used to secure the beam ends, as is customary in England.

FIG. —. ITALIAN TRAWL HEAD.

The following are the dimensions of the trawl heads exhibited at London. Height inside, or vertical diameter from top of shoe to lower part of beam, 2 feet 6½ inches; horizontal diameter, 3 feet 6 inches; shoe 4 inches by — inch iron; front of head, — inches by — inch iron; back, 1½ inches diameter.

The bridles were of four-stranded, 6½-inch manilla rope.

The trawl used on the smaller craft, and which is pulled in by hand or by means of a small winch, is of a peculiar pattern so far as the beam and trawl heads are concerned, the net itself having the same general appearance which is characteristic of this form of apparatus. The following is a description of one of these trawls exhibited at London.

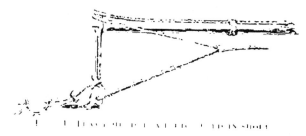

FIG. —. ITALIAN TRAWL BEAM AND HEADS IN SHOES.

The beam was 21 feet long, and 4 inches in diameter. In each end of it was fixed an iron bolt 3 or 4 inches long, which passed through a hole in the top of the head iron, and was prevented from getting out of its socket by a rope which was tightly stretched along the top of the beam and fastened at each end to the top of the head irons, one end of this rope being hauled tight by a small lanyard rove through roughly-made bulls eyes. The head piece is of a peculiar pattern and an idea of its form can best be obtained from the illustration (fig. 3). A broad lower part of sole curves up in front like the runner of a sled, but about four 5 inches above the ground the shoe is fixed to a round bar of iron 2 inches in diameter, which at the top is flattened slightly and perforated with two holes, one for the net rope and the other for the head rope. On the upper side of the sole or shoe is a eye, through which passes the ground rope, the end of which makes fast to the round part of the head iron. The sole is 4 foot long where it rests on the ground, made of 4 by 2½ inches flat iron. The head is 3 feet 5 inches from to the extreme top; the beam is raised about 2½ feet above the ground. The ground rope of this trawl is fitted with chain festoons in the same manner as the larger Belgian trawl.

In order to make this tow over the ground without upsetting, a short bridle or span is attached to each head iron. The lower part of this bridle (which is 4 feet 5 inches long, and well parcelled to prevent chafe), passes through a hole in the front part of the shoe, say 6 inches above the ground, being knotted on its end to prevent it from coming out; the upper part (5 feet 8 inches long) fastens round the head above the end of the beam. Beyond this span the bridle proper extends to the towing warp.

4. METHODS OF FISHING

The methods of working the trawls on the larger class of Belgian vessels, according to M. Loutrain, are the same as those employed on the English trawlers.

The "single boating" system is the only one followed, each vessel taking its own catch to market. Ice is carried for preserving the fish. The smack from Ostend usually make trips of eight to ten days in length, while the Heyst and Blankenberghe craft rarely stay out more than one or two days. The fish are packed in boxes on board the vessels and brought to market in baskets. All the fish caught by the Ostend boats are sold at that port, and from thence they are distributed by the dealers.

C. HOLLAND

The fisheries of Holland are of a mixed nature, differing from those of most English ports in that the same vessels which follow herring fishing for a portion of the year may at other times engage in beam trawling, or the beam trawler itself may be employed in fishing with long lines to-morrow. It is therefore somewhat difficult to say precisely what is the relative importance of beam trawling among the fisheries pursued by the Dutch. That it is an important branch of the fisheries of Holland is well known.

"Next to the herring fishery," says a Dutch writer, "the capture of fresh fish is the principal one in Holland. The fish are sometimes caught with hooks, but more frequently with trawls and other drag nets. In this fishery all the *bomschuiten* of the coast take part during the winter; and some of the luggers which carry on the herring fishery in summer; also the fifty large vessels referred to above (as being employed a portion of the year in fishing for cod with lines), and all sorts of other vessels, great and small, hailing from the small towns along the coast.*

Assuming that there is probable truth in the belief held by some writers that the use of beam-trawls was first made known to the English fishermen by the Dutch who accompanied the Prince of Orange to England in 1688, there is reason to believe that this system of fishing has long been practiced by the Netherlanders.

1. FISHING GROUNDS

While the larger vessels commonly fish in the North Sea, the *bomschuiten* usually carry on their work not far from the Dutch coast. Generally the Dutch vessels resort to many of the same grounds for trawling that are visited by the fishermen of the countries previously mentioned.

2. VESSELS

The larger class of vessels employed in beam-trawling are, as has been said, generally employed in herring fishing during the season when herring are most abundant in the North Sea. As the herring fishery is par excellence, the most important of all the Dutch fisheries, the vessels are constructed and rigged with especial reference to their fitness for catching herring, while their adaptability to beam-trawling is, in most cases, considered of secondary importance. These vessels— the so-called luggers or loggers—range from about 45 to 70 tons. They are not so sharp forward as the British smacks, are nearly of the same relative proportions as to length, breadth and depth, being possibly not quite so deep as the English craft. They are flush-decked, ketch or yawl rigged, and generally with mainmast arranged so that it can be lowered. They have an ordinary capstan that stands well aft—so as to be out of the way of the nets when herring fishing—and the trawl warp leads over the side abreast of this capstan. The winches "dummy," etc., that form a part of the deck equipment of a first-class English trawler were not attached to the models of Dutch vessels exhibited at Berlin, 1880 or London, 1883; therefore it may be assumed that these are not used.

The *bomschuiten* are a peculiar class of smaller fishing craft, designed especially for use on parts of the coast where harbors are not easy of access or where there are no harbors. They are made extraordinarily wide, being about two-thirds as broad as long, while the bottom is flat and constructed with especial reference to being hauled out on a beach or again launched through the surf. They are clinker built, usually about 30 feet long, both ends shaped nearly alike, rounding, yet almost

* Introduction to the general catalogue of the Netherlands exhibit at London, 1883.

square on top, have flush decks, and each carries a large capstan near the stern that is the motive power for getting on board two trawls which they use. They have a peculiar sort of trawling, supplemented occasionally by a small square topsail on the mainmast.

NETHERLANDS.

The beam trawls commonly used by the larger class of the Dutch vessels are about the same in all essential details as those used by English fishermen.

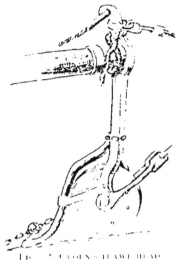

FIG.—COCK'S TRAWL HEAD.

A peculiar form of trawl head, Fig. 2, was exhibited in the Netherlands department at London 1883, by M. Cock, of Scheveningen. This was the invention of the exhibitor, and was attached to a trawl net designed for sole fishing such as is used by the *house trawl*, and which it is desirable to have pass easily over the ground. The idea is somewhat similar to that of de Caux's, but is less elaborate.

This trawl head is somewhat difficult to describe. The upper part is a square bar of iron, forked at the lower extremity to fit over the wheel, and having holes through the extremities for the axle of the wheel to pass through. The upper part of this iron is bent slightly backwards and broadened out somewhat to admit of holes being made in it; one for the end of the trawl beam iron and others for the bridle shackle and head rope. To the rear lower part is welded a sort of foot recurved extending over the back of the wheel and resting on the ground behind, being held in place by a stout U shaped iron clamp which passes round it and each end of which is bolted to the prongs of the head iron a little above the wheel axle. At the extremity of this foot on top is an eye for the ground rope of the trawl to pass through. The wheel itself is of hard wood, banded with iron, and at equal distances around it, near the edge, are a number of holes. These holes are so placed for the purpose of stopping the wheel from revolving, if deemed desirable, by shoving a key through the prong of the iron into any one of the holes that chances to be uppermost. A large shackle, one end of which is connected with the wheel by the axle bolt, comes in front of the wheel, and from this and the shackle at the top of the iron extends a short chain span that connects with a shackle at its end, to which also the bridle is attached. The following are some details of the measurements: Total height, 3 feet 1 inch; diameter of wheel, $11\frac{1}{2}$ inches; thickness of wheel, 5 inches: size of iron between wheel and beam, $1\frac{1}{2}$ by $1\frac{1}{2}$ inches; hole for beam iron, $1\frac{3}{4}$ by $\frac{5}{8}$ inches: lower part of foot is quite flat, $3\frac{1}{4}$ by $\frac{5}{8}$ inches; lower chain bridle, from axle of wheel, 2 feet 8 inches; upper bridle, 1 foot 10 inches.

In this case a flat bar of iron is fitted into the end of the beam (which is banded to prevent its splitting), and this iron, projecting beyond the beam, slips into an oblong hole at the upper part of the trawl-head.

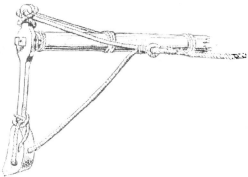

FIG. 33. DUTCH TRAWL-HEAD.

The trawls ordinarily used by the *bomschuiten* have some peculiarities. The following is a description of one of these trawls, exhibited at London, 1883: The beam is made of soft wood, $25\frac{1}{2}$ feet long, $3\frac{3}{4}$ inches in diameter, backed by a square iron bar $\frac{3}{4}$ inch square, which is seized to the beam. Projecting from the beam ends are iron bars which pass through the holes in the top of the head-irons. The head-iron is 3 feet high; it is straight, small at the top, but with a heavy square foot that is 10 inches high and 4 inches square, rounded on the lower front part so that it will slip over the bottom. (See Fig. 33.) Through this foot are two holes, one about in its center, from front to rear, for the lower part of the span to pass through, and the other transversely, near the lower extremity, for the ground rope to reeve through. The whole affair is simple and primitive. A rope span extends forward from the head, a large thimble being seized in its bight, and into this thimble is bent the bridle. One end of this span fastens to the upper part of the head-iron, and is 2 feet long; the other or lower part of the span is 2 feet 7 inches long, and passes through the foot of the head-iron and is held by a knot on the end of the rope.

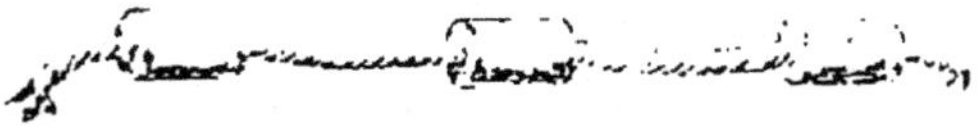

FIG. [illegible].—SECTION OF GROUND-ROPE.

The ground-rope is in striking contrast to those used by British fishermen. It is a small-sized hemp rope, scarcely larger than an inch, and on it are strung, at distances of 3½ inches between each two, a number of lead sinkers, these being 1½ inches long and 1 inch in diameter, with holes through them sufficiently large to admit the rope. (See Fig. [illegible].) The net itself does not differ materially from other trawl nets.

C. METHODS OF FISHING.

The methods of fishing with beam trawls on the larger Dutch vessels are essentially the same as those adopted by the English, so I am assured by Mr. A. E. Maas, of Scheveningen. Holdsworth says: "The same method of fishing is general on the coasts of Holland, Belgium, and France; but the Dutch are peculiar in using two trawls at once, one being towed from the bow and the other from the stern of the vessel."

It is a question, he thinks, whether, taking the year through, much advantage is gained from this system, although undoubtedly large catches are made by it sometimes. It is possibly true that, at the time Holdsworth wrote, the Dutch were not using the large beam trawls—a single trawl to a vessel—as they now do in the North Sea. His remark on the system of trawling pursued by the fishermen of the Netherlands applies more particularly to the *bomschuiten*, all of which, according to Mr. Maas, still use two trawls—each with a beam about 20 to 24 feet long, of the kind last described—one of which is put out from the stern and the other from the bow. The peculiar construction of the "*bomschuiten*" makes it possible for them to operate two trawls, though this might be found impracticable and unprofitable on vessels of the ordinary form. The "*bomschuiten*" are so modeled that when their lee boards are up they have a minimum of lateral resistance; therefore, when towing their gear, they slide off almost dead to leeward, drifting very much faster, of course, than a deeper vessel would. With a fresh breeze of wind and a lee tide effective work may be done; but with the tide running to windward it is difficult to understand how these boats can work to advantage.

All of the Dutch vessels take their own catch to market, and are what would be termed "single boaters" in England. The "*bomschuiten* rarely stay out more than a day or two, but the larger vessels make longer cruises, in most if not all cases bringing in a portion of their fish alive and the rest in ice.

D. GERMANY

Though trawling, in various forms, is quite extensively prosecuted by the Germans, beam-trawl fishing proper has not assumed very important proportions as compared with this fishery in some other countries.

1. FISHING GROUNDS

The German trawlers fish chiefly, if not wholly, in the North Sea but, as a rule, not far from their own coast. As the shore soundings off the west coast of Prussia constitute some of the best of the North Sea fishing grounds, more especially in summer, there is no need for the German vessels to go such long distances from home ports as the English trawlers often do. But since the larger trawling vessels often market their catch at English ports, they are placed in essentially the same position as the British trawlers, so far as nearness to fishing grounds is concerned. The small craft, of course, fish quite close to the land, but the larger vessels often go some distance off when the inshore fisheries are not profitable.

VESSELS

Among the most important types of beam trawlers from Germany may be mentioned the luggers or "loggers" of Emden and a peculiar ketch-rigged class of vessels that have been designed by Blankenese builders. The first named of these were like many of the Dutch trawlers, originally designed for the herring fishery, and in fact were either built in Holland or modeled after the vessels of that country. They are about 60 to 70 tons, rather full, flush-decked, and ketch-rigged, the lower masts being somewhat longer than those of the English smack, and the mizzen-mast a trifle farther forward.

The Blankenese-built vessels are of a similar rig, but are sharper, and provided with a well for keeping their fish alive. The striking peculiarity of this type of craft is the shape of its bottom. Though a keel vessel, the lower part of the bottom, which is about half the width of the deck, is nearly flat and sharp at each end, like the bottom of an American dory. This flat section has flaring sides that are 2 to 3 feet high and which are joined to the upper part of the hull, that is shaped like the top of an ordinary vessel. It is claimed that these vessels are swift and seaworthy, and that they have the special qualification of keeping their fish alive much longer than they can be kept in round-bottomed smacks.

Several forms of sharp-sterned decked boats are employed in trawling along the German coast, though this can not in any way be called beam trawling since the apparatus has no beam attached to it, and is most commonly operated by two boats working together, in a manner precisely similar to the method practiced by the Spanish fishermen for working the large bou net.[*]

APPARATUS.

The beam trawls used on the German vessels are the same as those employed by English fishermen, the latter having been taken as the standard.

METHODS OF FISHING.

The methods adopted by the Germans are like those of the English as might naturally be expected, when it is stated that fishermen from the east coast of England have been employed by German firms to act in the capacity of experts or instructors in this branch of the industries.

The vessels fish singly, each marketing its own catch, and on some occasions the fish have been sold in English ports.

E. SPAIN

The use of the beam trawl in Spain is, I think, of recent date, though other forms of trawls or drag nets have long been employed in that country.

One of the most common forms is worked by two boats, each of which is attached to and tows one wing of the net. This is used extensively on the Mediterranean coast of Spain. It is called a bou net, or sometimes a parella or parenzella.

Of late years, however, several screw steam trawlers have been built in Scotland for the Spanish fisheries. These are owned at San Sebastian. They are fine, seaworthy, ketch-rigged vessels of 60 to 70 tons and well adapted for beam trawling, which they carry on chiefly in the Bay of Biscay.

THE BOU NET, OR PARELLA.

It is believed that the parella, which is probably identical with the Italian parenzella, was invented in the sixteenth century. This name, according to Captain Constantini, means a pair in the Catalan language. It is applied to a plow that two oxen are required to work and likewise to this net, which is towed by two boats. The net has two long arms or wings the lower edges of which are weighted with small sinkers, while the upper edges are raised from the bottom, and, consequently, the mouth of the net is kept open by numbers of cork floats. The arms are 140 meshes, or about 3½ fathoms deep, the size of mesh being 2 inches, and 7 fathoms long, the cork rope and ground rope having nearly the same curve; the body of the net, from where it is joined by the wings, tapers so as to form a cone 11 yards long, which is joined by a small neck to the end, the extremity of which is flat and spread out considerably. This end corresponds to the cod-end of a beam trawl. To the end of each wing is attached a towing span, a double rope, distended in the middle with a wooden spreader or cross bar, one bight of which is secured to the extremity of the wing and the other bight having an eye for the towing rope to bend into. These nets are used in different depths, sometimes in as much as 400 fathoms. The towing warps are about 300 fathoms long. When the boats are towing the parella, they keep at a distance of 400 to 500 fathoms from each other, so that the arms of the apparatus will be well extended, that they may sweep a wide area of sea bottom.

The following are the dimensions of the parella, as given by Captain Commetma: total length about 40 fathoms, length of arms, each 7 fathoms, width of arms about 2 fathoms, or 130 meshes, size of mesh in arms, 2 inches, size of mesh in body of net, 1 inch and ⅜ of an inch. The lead sinkers weigh about 1 pound each, and are placed 18 inches apart on the ground rope.

The parella is used from October 20 to Easter Monday, during which season the various species of fish that occur near the bottom in the Mediterranean are captured.

Captain Commetma is authority for saying that the beam net is used by steamers on the north coast of Spain, two steamers towing the net. Trawling in this manner is, however, carried on only to a limited extent in the north of Spain, but very largely in sail boats in the Mediterranean.

III.—ATTEMPTS TO USE THE BEAM TRAWL IN THE FISHERIES OF THE UNITED STATES

Several attempts have been made to use beam trawls in the fisheries of the United States, as detailed in the following statements, and it is quite possible that similar trials have been made by other parties which I have no knowledge of. It will be noticed that the attempts alluded to here resulted in failure. The trial made off Cape Cod could scarcely be called a fair test of the apparatus, while Mr. Booth holds the opinion that a longer protracted test in the lakes, by a competent expert, might lead to far different results from those which he obtained in his experiment.

The following are the facts relative to the trials which have been made.

Capt. Sylvester Walen, of Boston, Mass., states that about 1864 Capt. Richard Leonard, a native of Ireland, but then fishing from Boston, had the schooner Salpa built on purpose for trying the experiment of fishing with a beam trawl off the New England coast. Captain Leonard visited Ireland and brought back with him sufficient apparatus for making the experiment. The trawl was tried off Cape Cod, but with no success, therefore that method of fishing had to be abandoned.

The captain and crew of the Salpa, says Captain Walen, instead of getting excellent results from this mode of fishing in American fisheries, kept their proposed experiments a profound secret, hoping not only to profit by being first in the field in this new enterprise, but also to avoid the antagonism of other fishermen not similarly provided.

Mr. J. H. McManus, of Boston, who was part owner of the *Sappho* at the time the experiment above referred to was tried, says she carried a beam trawl of the largest size, having a 50-foot beam; that it was set several times off Cape Cod in 10 to 20 fathoms of water, but no fish of any consequence, except flounders, was taken in it. The owners of the *Sappho*, all poor men, according to Mr. McManus, could not afford to continue the trials. Therefore the attempt to use this form of apparatus was given up, and the three trawls which had been brought over from England were sold to parties in Virginia to use for some unknown purpose in Chesapeake Bay.

Mr. McManus thinks that possibly one cause of this failure to introduce the beam trawl was due to the boats not being properly equipped for that purpose, but he is, nevertheless, of the opinion that it can be used to good advantage north of Cape Cod.

Mr. A. Booth, of Chicago, well known throughout the United States as an extensive packer of fish and oysters, told me while at London in 1883 that he imported a beam trawl from England as early as 187[illegible], and tried to use it for the capture of whitefish (*Coregonus*) on Lake Michigan, but although a few were taken the attempt was a failure, as the trawl could not be successfully used there because it became frequently entangled with the sunken logs that were more or less numerous on the bottom of the lake. He also stated that he had no experienced man in this particular fishery to handle his trawl, and, hence, he is not fully satisfied that it is impracticable to use this form of apparatus in some of the lake fisheries.

In the scientific investigations made by the U. S. Fish Commission off the Atlantic coast from Cape Hatteras to Halifax, Nova Scotia, the beam trawl has been extensively used, and among the various species of fish that have been captured in it may be mentioned the flounder (*Glyptocephalus cynoglossus*), which was first taken on the New England coast in 1877. This species, which for food purposes is pronounced quite equal to the European sole, has a very small mouth, and can therefore be taken in large numbers only in a beam trawl. It occurs in greater or less abundance off the New England coast and northwardly to the Grand Bank.

Lieutenant Commander Z. L. Tanner, who has for several years been in command of the Fish Commission's steamers, has used the beam trawl very extensively for scientific purposes in the waters of Massachusetts Bay and off Cape Cod, as well as elsewhere along the coast. He says that there are large areas on the eastern slope of Stellwagen Bank, and east of Cape Cod, outside of a depth of 15 fathoms, where a beam trawl could be employed to advantage, the bottom being a mixture of and mud. These localities are noted for an abundance of that fish, among which the pole flounder occurs in large numbers. He believes it would be entirely practicable to carry on beam-trawling in those waters, but thinks it would be necessary to have a steam capstan to get the gear up.

The peculiar form of trawl net which is used in the Mediterranean is successfully worked in the waters off the west coast of the United States.

Prof. David S. Jordan, who investigated the Pacific coast fisheries in 1879, so writing of the Italian fishermen of San Francisco, Cal., says that in 1875 the paranzella was introduced in the fisheries of that port. The fishermen of other nationalities threatened to burn up these nets and the boats used when the nets were employed. San Francisco is the only place in this country where this style of fishing has been introduced. There were two antagonistic companies who used these nets; they have now consolidated and divide the profits equally. Each company has three boats and employs twelve or thirteen men, one of whom is constantly engaged in selling fish in the market. The stock is owned chiefly by men not actually engaged in fishing. This is divided irregularly, one man owning a net, another a boat, etc. Out of the gross profits are paid first, the entire expenses, including provisions of the men; next the boats and nets, etc. The remainder is divided into shares, one share to each boat, one to each actual fisherman, and one-half share to each net actually in use. In these two companies, there being six boats, two nets, and twenty-five men, the whole is divided into thirty-two shares. The captain sometimes received one and one-fourth shares.

IV.—POSSIBILITIES OF SUCCESSFULLY USING THE BEAM-TRAWL IN THE SEA-FISHERIES OF THE UNITED STATES.

So far as the ocean-fisheries of the United States are concerned, more especially on the Atlantic coast, there is little probability that the beam-trawl will be employed for some time to come, chiefly for the following reasons. First, many parts of the fishing grounds, now most commonly frequented, are not suitable for beam-trawling, being too rough, and in many localities the water is too deep; second, our most valuable ground fish—cod, haddock, halibut, etc.—occur in such abundance that far greater catches can generally be obtained with lines or gill-nets than it would be possible to get in a beam-trawl, and as bait can usually be obtained at a moderate outlay, the lack of this is not an inducement, as it is in Europe, to adopt beam-trawling; third, the flat fishes—several species of flounders, dabs, etc.—that occur off the east coast of

Though it is true that the larger part of the best fishing grounds are too rough for beam-trawling, it is nevertheless certain that there are extensive areas where trawls can be used, and should at least not be in this ever be introduced into the fisheries of the United States; no doubt it will be found that grounds now little frequented may prove unexpected storehouses of wealth so far as fish-life is concerned.

the United States and for the capture of which the beam trawl is more specially adapted, are now of comparatively little value in our markets, and half a ton of them would scarcely bring as much as is obtained in London for a hundred pounds of soles.

The following statement of the arrivals of fishing vessels at Boston Mass., in a single day, and the quantity of cod or haddock or cod on board of each, shows what enormous captures of these fish are sometimes made with trawl lines. When it is understood that these catches of fish are often taken in a single day, and that a vessel seldom fishes longer than two or three days consecutively, it will be apparent enough that like results can not be obtained by using beam trawls. Schooner *Mabel Kennison*, Georges, 40,000 pounds haddock. Schooner *Emily P. Wright*, Georges, 40,000 pounds haddock. Schooner *Gertie L. Mason*, Le Have, 30,000 pounds haddock and cod. Schooner *C. J. French*, Georges, 15,000 pounds haddock. Schooner *Hattie L. Phillips*, Georges, 75,000 pounds haddock. Schooner *Carrie d'Anne*, Georges, 60,000 pounds haddock. Schooner *Rebecca Bartlett*, Georges, 15,000 pounds haddock. Schooner *Henry W. Longfellow*, Georges, 60,000 pounds haddock. Schooner *Thos Parsons*, Georges, 60,000 pounds haddock. Schooner *Delia*, Georges, 40,000 pounds haddock. Schooner *Haskell*, Georges, 50,000 pounds haddock. Schooner *J. L. Colleaton*, Georges, 35,000 pounds haddock. Schooner *Mystic*, Georges, 40,000 pounds had dock. Schooner *Charles P. Lewiston*, Georges, 40,000 pounds. Schooner *Lorina L. Haskell*, Georges, 60,000 pounds haddock. Schooner *Ira dragon*, Georges, 40,000 pounds haddock. Schooner *Senator*, Georges, 30,000 pounds haddock. Schooner *J. W. Campbel*, Georges, 15,000 pounds haddock. Schooner *J. L. Garland*, Georges, 60,000 pounds haddock. Schooner *Clytie*, Georges, 15,000 pounds haddock. Schooner *Rebecca Bartlett*, Georges, 50,000 pounds haddock. Schooner *Edward Everett*, Georges, 60,000 pounds haddock. Schooner *Matched Arms*, Georges, 50,000 pounds haddock. Schooner *Isaac Allerton*, Georges, 40,000 pounds cod. Schooner *H. B. Winchester*, Georges, 60,000 pounds haddock. Schooner *Andrew Grimes*, Georges, 40,000 pounds had dock. Schooner *Isaac W. Freeman*, Georges, 60,000 pounds haddock. Schooner *Annie B.*, Georges, 40,000 pounds haddock. Schooner *Sarah C. Wharf*, Ipswich Bay, 15,000 pounds cod. Schooner *Grace L. Curtis*, Georges, 25,000 pounds haddock. Schooner *Laura Leavitt*, Georges, 50,000 pounds haddock. Schooner *Mary E. Curtis*, Georges, 50,000 pounds haddock. Schooner *W. Parnell O'Hara*, Georges, 40,000 pounds haddock. Schooner *Canton Dove*, Georges, 15,000 pounds haddock. Schooner *New England*, Georges, 15,000 pounds haddock. Schooner *Ethel Maud*, Georges, 15,000 pounds haddock. Schooner *Eben Scott*, Georges, 15,000 pounds haddock. Schooner *John Winthrop*, Georges, 40,000 pounds haddock. Schooner *Charles L. Lawrence*, Georges, 50,000 pounds haddock. Schooner *Reporter*, Georges, 15,000 pounds haddock. Schooner *Phil Sheridan*, Georges, 60,000 pounds haddock. Schooner

Greta Lufae Georges, 18,000 pounds haddock. Schooner *Edith Emery* Georges, 60,000 pounds haddock.[1]

It is therefore evident that, with such conditions prevailing, the beam trawl can not be profitably employed off the Atlantic coast even supposing extraordinary catches could be taken in it. However should the demand for that fish increase in the future, which is extremely probable, it will doubtless be found that beam trawling can be prosecuted off our eastern shores with profit and success, while in a country having such a vast extent of sea-coast as the United States has, and such varied fisheries it is impossible to say what may not be done with an apparatus which is so effective as is the beam trawl for the capture of ground-fish. The fact that the *paranzella* has been profitably employed on the Pacific coast is a matter of interest in this connection and indicates that there may be in that region an opportunity to use the beam trawl which is a much more effective form of apparatus.

[1] See Report United States Fish Commission, Georges and Le Have fisheries as to cod and halibut, and where they were caught.

INDEX

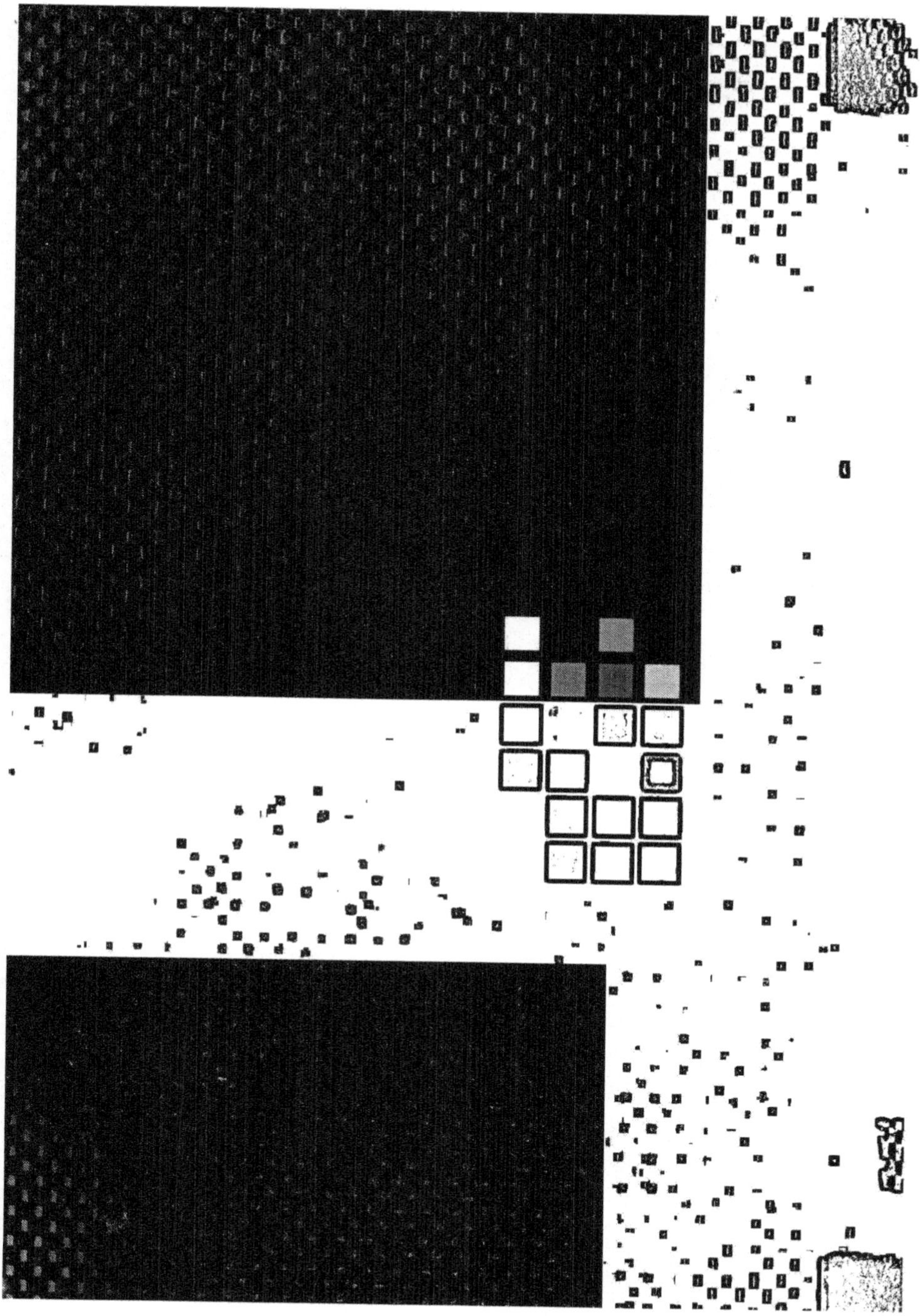

CPSIA information can be obtained
at www.ICGtesting.com
Printed in the USA
LVOW05s1525110517
534153LV00010BA/202/P